GW00392033

Walks in the Dartmoor National Park

The Dart Valley

Including 2½ inch 1:25000 maps

No 3 in the Dartmoor National Park Authority's Walks booklets series.

For general information enquiries about the National Park send a large stamped and addressed envelope to:

The Information Officer,
Dartmoor National Park Authority,
Parke,
Haytor Road,
Bovey Tracey,
Newton Abbot,
Devon.
TQ13 9JQ.

Tel: Bovey Tracey (0626) 832093.

Original text prepared in the National Park Department by Gail Shepheard, edited by Elizabeth Prince. This edition edited by John Weir with further assistance from Chris Hart, Gillian Taylor and Mike Perriam. The Department wishes to acknowledge the help of many local people in the research for this booklet.

All photographs by John Weir except Chris Chapman photographs on pp. 14 (top), 29, 31, 44 and 60.
John Head — Cover.

This edition first published in Great Britain in 1990 by Devon Books.
Copyright © Dartmoor National Park Department 1990
ISBN: 0 86114-861-4
All rights reserved.
Typeset by P&M Typesetting Ltd, Exeter, Devon EX1 1UG
Printed and bound in Great Britain by Penwell Print Ltd, Callington.

DEVON BOOKS
Official Publisher to Devon County Council
An imprint of Wheaton Publishers Ltd,
a member of Maxwell Communication Corporation plc.

Wheaton Publishers Ltd,
Hennock Road, Marsh Barton, Exeter, Devon EX2 8RP
Tel: 0392 411131

SALES
Direct sales enquiries to Devon Books at the address above.

INTRODUCTION

The walks in this booklet are based partly on Public Rights of Way, partly on common land, partly on areas of enclosed moorland (newtakes) where walkers have been granted access by the landowners and tenant farmers, and partly on other areas of public access.

Each of the walks described has been chosen with an eye to the attractiveness of the countryside and also the features of local interest.

Since it started in 1963, the Ranger Service of the Dartmoor National Park Authority has been clearing, signposting and, where necessary, waymarking Rights of Way in the National Park. By its nature this work is never complete, but all paths described in this booklet have received attention and walkers should not encounter any difficulty.

Public footpaths and bridleways are an important part of the overall system of highways and byways in an area. On the map pages in this booklet (scale used 1:25000 2½ inches to 1 mile) all the Rights of Way in the area have been included as they appear on the County Definitive Map of Public Paths, with only minor changes in cases amended subsequently, and where arrangements have been made.

Please remember that footpaths and bridleways run over private land. Some pass through the middle of farmyards. Whenever in the countryside please follow the Country Code, in particular fasten all gates, keep dogs under proper control and take your litter home.

Comments and further suggestions about these walks are welcomed.

NATIONAL PARKS

The far-sighted National Parks and Access to the Countryside Act, 1949, led to ten areas in England and Wales being given special protection as National Parks. In 1989 similar status was given to the Broads. All have one vital feature in common – they encompass beautiful country which is relatively wild, unspoilt and sparsely populated. Each National Park Authority has a duty to preserve and enhance the area's natural beauty, to promote its enjoyment and to have regard for its social and economic well being.

The Dartmoor National Park Authority carries out these tasks through its role as a planning authority and through its powers derived from various Acts of Parliament relating to the countryside. A National Park Plan (1977) and its Review set out the Authority's objectives and policies and the ways and means employed to achieve them.

ABOUT THE LAND AND RIGHTS OF WAY

The designation of a National Park in no way alters the land use or land ownership pattern. All the land is owned by someone – whether an individual, or a public or private body. Even common land has owners, and registered commoners also have an interest in its welfare. Most of the open land is common over which farmers living on and around the moor have common rights – principally to graze their livestock. People have always walked and ridden on Dartmoor's commons and this practice was legalised in 1985 by the Dartmoor Commons Act. This Act also provided a basis for drawing up byelaws to regulate public use of the commons and it set up the Dartmoor Commoners' Council to regulate the agricultural use of the commons.

There are certain moorland areas, some very large, that were enclosed by dry-stone walls during the latter part of the 18th and earlier part of the 19th centuries. These are not subject to commoners' rights, being generally let to tenant farmers. This distinction is important since the custom of walkers' access over unfenced common does not apply to these enclosures, which are known as newtakes. It can be taken as a rule of thumb, when walking on Dartmoor, that newtakes and other enclosed areas are not open to walkers by *legal* right. However, in some areas Access Agreements and permitted paths have been negotiated by the National· Park Authority thus allowing for public access on a more formal basis.

Off the commons and on the enclosed land, Public Rights of Way are all important. These allow walkers to traverse beautiful countryside and to make intriguing discoveries without disturbing the work of farmers. The Rights of Way are protected and maintained by the Dartmoor National Park Authority which relies on the help and co-operation of all walkers.

To make paths accessible and to avoid risk of trespass, the National Park Authority has cleared, signposted and waymarked all the paths used in this booklet. Signposts normally mark the beginning or junction of paths, and waymarking, (yellow spots for public footpath and blue spots for public bridlepath) is used where the path is not otherwise obvious. Where paths pass through farmyards please be careful to go straight through, staying on the line of the path.

On open moorland, signposts and waymarks have been omitted to avoid intrusion in the landscape. If a path is not clear on the ground, follow the route description carefully in conjunction with the map so that the right direction is taken. The paths have been drawn to show exactly where the correct route goes, for example, which side of the hedge, or at what angle it crosses a field. Contour lines are not shown in order to allow greater clarification of the other map information. Generally speaking, where the route is clear on the ground, less detail is given in the route descriptions.

In the text, path directions are printed in colour to enable the walker to distinguish more easily the directions from the purely descriptive or interpretive material. The letters '(R)' and '(L)' mean 'to the right' and 'to the left'.

Beside the title of each walk are the page numbers where the relevant maps are to be found. The paths on these maps are all numbered and classified according to which parish they lie in. Thus BW4 means Buckfastleigh West path 4. The initials used to denote parishes are:-

A	Ashburton		**L**	Lydford
B	Buckfastleigh		**M**	Manaton
BW	Buckfastleigh West		**W**	Widecombe
H	Holne			

On the map (scale 1:25000 2½" to 1 mile) all public footpaths and bridlepaths are shown. Minor diversions are currently being undertaken on a few paths. Footpaths, bridlepaths, permitted routes and Unclassified County Roads are shown on the map as follows:-

-------------------------------------- *public footpath*	································· *permitted route*
— — — — — — — — — *public bridlepath*	_____ *Unclassified County Road*

The Unclassified County Roads shown on the maps are unmetalled, and always unsuitable for vehicles.

ADVICE TO WALKERS

General

Paths are often wet in parts so be prepared for this. During the summer, bracken can be so dominant that a few paths are likely to be slightly overgrown for a short period of time. However, while it can be unpleasant walking through bracken after heavy rain, paths are never impassable.

Some paths cross diagonally over fields which may be under cultivation. A walker is *legally* correct in following the path line across the crops. Groups of walkers should keep to a single line as walking several abreast will damage crops. Please make sure that all gates are shut behind you.

The approximate times needed to do these walks have been calculated from an average walking speed of 1½ miles (2.4 km) per hour.

Rivers and Stepping Stones

It is the convention when speaking of the banks of a river to name them right and left bank as if looking down river.

River banks on enclosed land are not rights of way, although some, of course, do have footpaths or bridleways running along parts of them. You may sometimes see anglers fishing from the banks; they will have purchased a permit which gives them access to that particular stretch of water for fishing. When a public path does run close to a river, please pass anglers quietly and do not disturb the water.

There are several walks in this booklet (from Dunnabridge, Dartmeet and Postbridge) that involve crossing stepping stones. A WARNING is given in the heading to each walk. THESE STEPPING STONES ARE NOT ALWAYS PASSABLE DURING OR AFTER HEAVY RAIN. However, the stones can quickly re-cover after a heavy shower.

In the interests of safety great care should be taken at all times. Even when the stepping stones are uncovered they may be slippery and a good sense of balance is needed to cross.

Transport and Parking

The starting points of some walks in this booklet can be reached by bus. Details cannot be given here as routes, periods of operation, and times can vary from year to year. Up-to-date information can be obtained from any National Park Information Centre or by phoning local bus stations in Exeter, Plymouth or Newton Abbot.

For people using their own cars to reach the start of a walk, it will be helpful to look at the brief introduction to the relevant starting point where parking facilities are described.

Please remember that it is an offence to park more than 15 yds from the road onto the common or to drive or park on a public footpath or bridleway. Please do not block field gates as farmers may need to use them.

6   **Early morning mist, the Dart Valley.**

POSTBRIDGE

The medieval clapper bridge, which spans the East Dart River a few yards downstream from the road bridge, is the main feature of Postbridge. Bridges like this, built with massive unhewn slabs of granite, are found over many of the rivers and streams of Dartmoor, this one being larger and better preserved than the others.

Major works to safeguard the clapper bridge and its surrounding area were undertaken early in 1975 by the Dartmoor National Park Authority and Devon County Council. The river was undermining the bank and it was noticed that one of the piers had begun to lean. The bank was rebuilt with a facing of large boulders (this technique has since been successfully used on other river-banks). One clapper stone was only just bearing on its pier, so, with scaffolding and jacks, it was raised very slightly to allow room for the top section of the pier to be re-formed. An epoxy resin jointing compound was used to make a waterproof bond between the stones while leaving the appearance unaltered.

The earliest known track to cross the East Dart using this clapper ran from Chagford to Tavistock. Documentary evidence lies in a detailed plan dated 1675. This appeared in John Ogilby's 'Britannia Depicta' which could be called the first road atlas of England. The track is shown as part of one from Exeter to Truro, and many landmarks are included, especially bridges on all the rivers. The clapper at Postbridge is marked "Post Stone Bridge, 3 arches".

In 1772 two Acts of Parliament formed the Tavistock and the Moretonhampstead Turnpike Trusts. The old track was subsequently improved and re-aligned to by-pass Chagford and go straight to Exeter. To recoup the money invested in

Postbridge, clapper and road bridge.

making this improved track, toll houses and turnpikes were built at certain points along it, one of the sites chosen being Postbridge. An inn was also built to offer refreshments to the traveller.

From 1780 agricultural 'improvers' obtained grants to enclose large areas of moorland. At Postbridge, two brothers, Thomas and John Hullet, enclosed an estate of 3,000 acres (1,214 hectares). The tin mines of Vitifer and Golden Dagger, about 3 miles (5 km) to the north east, in their turn also changed the face of the land. Some of the miners were housed at Postbridge; the settlement at Postbridge developed and in 1868 the Mission Chapel of St. Gabriel was built to serve the community.

Today Postbridge has, as well as an Inn (not the original), a Post Office and Village Stores. Near the Post Office is a large car park with public conveniences, and from Easter to the end of October a Dartmoor National Park Information Centre is open every day.

An infrequent local bus service operates in the area – 'phone local bus stations at Exeter or Plymouth for further details.

MAP
PAGE
72

POSTBRIDGE – BELLEVER BRIDGE, return via DURY – LYDGATE.

3¾ miles (6 km), about 2½ hours. A gentle walk through farm land and moorland. Part of the route, where it passes through fields, is not a registered Right of Way and is only used by kind permission of the landowners and tenant farmers. It is possible the fields may contain a bull. There is a small stream to ford on the return route. Paths used L18, L17.

From the car park walk down the main road towards the clapper bridge and turn right through the gate just before reaching the bridge onto Path L18. Follow the wall (R); a grassy path climbing the hill can be seen straight ahead. Go through the hunting gate and climb steeply between gorse bushes onto this path. Looking back there is a view of the clapper bridge and the East Dart valley to Broad Down (L) and Hartland Tor (R) with Sittaford Tor beyond. Just before the hunting gate is an old mould stone and nearby is the site of a former tin miners' barracks. The path can be clearly seen until near the road to Bellever, which it joins at an angle. The plantations here are part of the large Bellever Forest owned by the Forestry Commission; the bulk of the area was planted between 1935 and 1938. Looking to the skyline (L) you may see the distinctive shape of Haytor Rocks with Saddle Tor and Rippon Tor (R); these tors lie on the eastern edge of the moors. The view ahead is of Corndon Tor where there are several prehistoric cairns (heaps of stones marking burial sites) and along the ridge to Yar Tor (R) which overlooks Dartmeet.

Continue along the grass verge beside the road to Bellever. The surrounding area has greatly altered in appearance since the Forestry Commission bought it in 1931; then there was only a small plantation to the south of Bellever. The area you have just walked through was once one large newtake, Lakehead Hill, extending westwards over the hill to the main road. The road here was a rough forestry road until after the houses (L) were built in 1947 originally for forestry workers. It is now a County road.

Ahead in the sheltered hollow were the farms of Bellaford and Lake, two of the 'ancient tenements'. Thirty-five ancient tenements have been identified on Dartmoor. They are believed to have been founded sometime before the 13th century. The farms lie within the East and West Dart valleys. At the fork in the road go left to Bellever Bridge. Approaching the bridge, notice a line of stones standing at the edge of the road (R); on closer examination notice that the second stone has a 'C' cut into the face. This is a County stone which in the 19th century marked the amount of road maintained by the County this side of the County-built bridge (the rest of the road was the responsibility of the local people). There is another solitary County stone (L) on the bend beyond the bridge.

Just below the road bridge are the remains of a clapper bridge. The middle span is believed to have been built of wood, which had the advantage of being easily replaced if damaged or destroyed by flood.[1] This bridge was first used by inhabitants of the surrounding ancient tenements when they followed the Lich Path across the moors to their parish church at Lydford.

Beyond the bridge turn left from the road and follow the bank of the Dury Brook up stream from its confluence with the East Dart River. Bear right as you

Bellever Clapper Bridge.

pass in front of Dury Farm (another ancient tenement), and right again up the farm track.

Take the first gate on the left; the gate marks where moorland becomes farmland and it should be securely shut. Other gates ahead are just as important as they divide the fields of different farms. This path is not a Public Right of Way, though the farmer has given permission for people to follow it to where they join the registered path. Walkers should be aware that the farmer may need to use these fields to run a bull.

Follow the wall (R) to the pile of rocks (field clearance boulders) then bear slightly right, cutting the corner of the field, to a sunken lane lined by large gorse bushes. The track (signposted) turns sharp left and descends. At the bottom turn sharp left again before reaching another waste rock heap. You have now joined the bridleway L17 which leads from Pizwell (R). **Pizwell, now one farm, was originally 3 ancient tenements, the buildings were all situated together and the land was divided up into blocks of fields each belonging to a different tenement.**

In the 17th century during a tithe dispute it was stated that the inhabitants of these farms were rich, and that the ground was good and was tilled with oats, rye and barley. Wheat has been grown on some of the ancient tenements within living memory.

Continuing, on L17 now, you will soon find yourself following a line of boulders which becomes the left-hand wall of a downward running lane. **The piles of rocks you have passed are just a few of those dragged out of the ground; this operation is only worthwhile where there is a good depth of soil for cultivation. The farmers have little use for these particular rocks but the National Park Authority has taken some to repair eroded river banks.** At the bottom, bend right but keep well to the left of the track as the river now flows along this section. Cross the Dury Brook on a single stone clapper bridge to the gate beyond.

The track continues as a sunken way. Bend left when two gateways ahead are seen and then right following the wall (R). Pass through a hunting gate beside a row of young beech trees. Follow the wall (R) and when three-quarters of the way across the field turn downhill passing below a summer hut and through another hunting gate.

Walking on the level now, cross the next field and beyond the next hunting gate follow the low wall (L) until it ends then follow the wall now on your right, to the gate below Lydgate.

In these small fields, known as plats (plots), there is very little depth of soil and it would be unprofitable to cultivate the area, Lydgate is not an ancient tenement and has probably been settled within the last 200 years.

Secure the gate then cross the forecourt area and continue along the unmetalled road. About 50 yards (46m) past the gate turn off left downwards to the river keeping the fence on your left. This path is not a right of way but the owners have given permission for people to follow it along the bank of the river. Go through the gate in the next fence and over the clapper bridge from where the car park is only a few paces up the main road.

(4 miles [6.5km], about 2¾ hours. WARNING: there are natural, STEPPING STONES across the East Dart River. If the walk is attempted after rain and the stones are covered then you must retrace your outward route. For information on rivers and stepping stones, see page 5. This walk passes through enclosed moorland [newtakes]. The return route following the Powerdermills Leat is not a registered Right of Way and is used by the kind permission of the land-owners and tenant farmers. As it is only a permitted path it is possible that the fields may contain a bull. Nowhere steep, but over rough, often wet ground. Advisable to wear good walking shoes or boots. Paths used L6, L44).

From the Postbridge car park follow the main road (B3212) over the bridge. The path L6 starts at a hunting gate (L), adjacent to a 5 bar gate. Pass through this gate and a similar gate ahead. The path runs around two sides of this field, following the wall (R) towards Ringhill, then turn left and follow the wall to the river, passing Hartyland (R).

The original settlement at Hartyland was where Jonas Coaker, known by local people as the Dartmoor Poet, was born in 1801, and he died at neighbouring Ringhill in 1890. He told, in verse, of unusual events on Dartmoor and of the doings of his neighbours. Not only did he work as a builder of newtake walls but he was also collector of rates for the parish of Lydford (once one of the most extensive parishes in the country) and one time landlord of the Warren House Inn serving Vitifer tin mines.[2]

Go through a hunting gate and continue near the river, passing through another two hunting gates in the small plantation near Hartyland into Hartland Tor Newtake. The path runs straight up the East Dart River Valley close to the river bank passing below Hartland Tor. Approaching the far side of the newtake, a wall (L) runs at an angle from the riverbank to the stile (keep above this wall as the ground below is boggy).

Cross the stile and you are now in the extensive Stannon Tor Newtake. Continue near the river until the valley widens and a tributary stream flows in from the north.

A short distance up the left* bank of the stream are the remains of the 'beehive hut', a small, domed structure of stone. Tinners are believed to have built it to store their tools in; the stones would have been covered with earth, and plants would have grown on top to give the appearance of an old spoil heap.[3]

Returning to the confluence, on the right* bank of the East Dart a deep, dry channel can be seen (opposite); this is the take off point of a leat and the start of the return route. The river can be forded by using the 'stepping stones' here.

* It is the convention to always name the banks of the river 'right' and 'left' as seen when looking DOWN river.

11

This leat was built to serve a gunpowder factory situated about halfway between Two Bridges and Postbridge and called Powder Mills. Here, gunpowder was produced by the Plymouth and Dartmoor Powder Co. from 1844 until the end of the 19th century. The gunpowder factory was an important employer of full-time and casual workers at a time when tin mining was on the decline. The leat bed you are walking beside brought water to power the mills.

Follow the leat for 1 mile (1.6 km). Each newtake has stockproof stiles so dogs will need assistance over. This path is not a public Right of Way though the farmer has given permission for people to follow the route along the leat. Walkers should be aware however that the farmer may need to use these newtakes to run a bull.

There is a good view of Hartland Tor across the valley. At one point a wall (R) runs beside the leat. The hill is steep here and the wall was built to protect sheep from injury in the leat. There are also occasional slabs of granite laid across the leat to enable the sheep to cross.

You will reach the Drift Lane L44 where it crosses the leat by means of a 9 slab bridge. The Drift Lane is used when driving stock between the farms and the moorland. At the bridge turn left down a short length of sunken lane which soon fords the Broadun Brook and, within a short distance, the Archerton Brook. Bear slightly right up over the rise, the track then gradually approaches the newtake wall (L). Further on pass through the gate by the end of the shelterbelt and continue to the main road. The Drift Lane here is wide and straight. Nearing the road there is a stile (L) which leads directly to the car park.

MAP PAGES 72, 73, 74, 75

POSTBRIDGE – RUNNAGE BRIDGE – CATOR GATE SHERRIL – DARTMEET, return via BRIMPTS – BABENEY – LAUGHTER HOLE – BELLEVER

11 miles (17.7 km), about 7 hours. A walk over farmland and moorland with very fine views. An alternative return route is given from Dartmeet should the river be low and the stepping stones on the East Dart River passable. Paths used: L15, W20, W26, W25, L26, L25, L18.

From Postbridge car park turn left along the road (B3212) and cross the bridge. Continue along the verge passing the East Dart Hotel (R). Continue on past the church. The church (R) was erected in 1868 as the Mission Chapel of St. Gabriel and was also used as the day school.

Take the second lane right (L15) after the church. Wesley House was until a few years ago a Methodist Chapel. Pass a turning (R) and another one (L), and soon you reach Lower Merripit. Merripit is one of the ancient tenements and dates from at least 1344 when the name is first mentioned in existing records.

Continue through the gate into the farmyard (it can be muddy). Passing the house (L), leave at the right-hand gate by the barn. Follow the hedge (L) to the stream, the Dury Brook, and beyond follow the track to the gate onto the road.

12

Here turn right to Runnage Bridge which spans the Walla Brook. The Walla Brook, along its entire length, forms part of the boundary of the Forest of Dartmoor.

Runnage, an ancient tenement dating from at least 1304, can be seen (L). Pizwell will soon come into view (R); it was originally a settlement of three tenements and still has the appearance of a small village. Pizwell and Babeny (seen on the return route) are thought to have been the first ancient tenements founded. In 1260 the inhabitants of 'Pushyll' and 'Balbeny' were granted permission by the Bishop Bronescombe to attend Widecombe Church rather than their parish church at Lydford, over 12 miles (19 km) away, on the west side of Dartmoor.

Cross the bridge and continue along the road. The plantation on Soussons Down (L) was planted by the Forestry Commission between 1947 and 1949. The footpath starts opposite a forest gateway about halfway between Runnage Bridge and Ephraim's Pinch. The story behind the name Ephraim's Pinch involves a young man named Ephraim who laid a wager that he could carry a sack of corn from Widecombe to Postbridge without dropping it. He reached the hill beyond the plantation but the 'pinch' was too much and he had to drop the sack. There is a more romantic version which says that he did it for the hand in marriage of a young lady and that he completed the task, but dropped dead when her father still said no.

The ground (R) is rough moorland and the line of the parish boundary (roughly parallel to the road) is marked by a row of gorse bushes and trees. The path crosses the boundary where it is at its closest to the road near a bond stone. The incised 'C.B.' stands for Cator Boundary; the land beyond is Cator Common. Just to the left and set back off the road is a fine prehistoric retaining circle. Passing from Manaton into Widecombe the path becomes W20, a sunken track running in a SSE direction. Cross over the Pizwell track and go through the gate.

With the help of the map you can see that a large area (L), as far as Blackaton, is laid out in a geometrical form uncommon on Dartmoor. Grendon Estate, in Spitchwick Manor, and Blackaton, then the manor of Blagdon Pipard, were sold by auction in the 1860s to Frederick Hand Firth J.P. of Essex. He altered the appearance of the whole area by new fencing and drainage, and by the planting of shelterbelts which became known as Grendon Strips. These can be seen (L) as a long line of trees which is, in fact, bisected by a road. The track (W20) meets the road at the strips. Pass through the gate and turn left along the road past the turning to Cator Court.

Cator is one of the 'vills' with Venville rights, i.e. situated outside the Forest of Dartmoor whereon it has grazing (and other) rights. It is believed that these rights were exercised before Dartmoor was made a Forest.

Going through Cator Gate, now removed, you reach the northern edge of Corndon. There were once numerous gates around the edge of the moor, and also between the Commons. The advent of motorised transport and the visitor caused them to be replaced by cattlegrids. It was once the pastime of the local youngsters to open these gates for approaching vehicles in the hope of a tip.

The footpath W26 starts at a rough road (R). The path soon turns off (L) along a sunken track, losing a little height, and then ascends gently. The track becomes wider and the Right of Way bears left ahead onto the smaller, worn path above.

Sherril

Dartmeet Bridge. If the water level is much higher than this on the middle pier, then take the alternative return route described later in this walk to avoid crossing any stepping stones.

Riddon, another ancient tenement, lies beyond the Walla Brook, just within the Forest. 'Walla' is derived from the Saxon 'Wealas' meaning foreigners or strangers. It is believed that the Celts were living in these high valleys (there are several Walla Brooks) when the Saxons settled.

The track passes beside the top walls of some fields, bending left, and descends to Sherril. Sherril is another of the farms (like Cator mentioned earlier) with Venville rights and is of a similar early date. On the gate the name is spelt in the old way, 'Sherwell', although it is always pronounced "Sherril".

Turn right onto the road and left over a stile after passing Sherril. The path W25 runs straight across this field to the gate opposite. In the next field follow the wall and fence (L) until you reach the stile and footbridge. The path then climbs with the wall (R) to Yar Tor Down. This moorland area abounds with prehistoric remains including fields, hut circles, cairns etc., but few of them are visually impressive. Just beyond the gate, on the left, two hut circles can be found and there are tumbled down walls of small enclosures.

From here the path is not obvious – head along the side of the hill overlooking the East Dart River and lose height slowly. Most of the hillside is covered in bracken but the clitter is nearer the tor so it is not too rough.

As you approach Dartmeet, the cafe, Badger's Holt, can be seen below. Still on the moorland, the path joins a track which passes above the buildings. Beyond the cafe the path descends to the car park at Dartmeet. Just beyond the car park but before the road bridge are the remains of a clapper bridge. This bridge was in use until 1826 when a violent thunderstorm on the 4th August caused the river to swell enormously and it was partly washed away. It was restored at the end of the century but was destroyed again within a few years.

WARNING. From Dartmeet there is a choice of return route depending on the state of the river; if the stepping stones are passable then take L26 and L25 via Brimpts and Babeny; if they are not passable then take L18 via Huccaby Cottage. Both routes meet at Laughter Hole Farm.

To judge if the stones are passable compare the photograph with the cut water on the middle pier of the road bridge at Dartmeet. If the river level is not much higher it is safe to cross.

If the stones on the Brimpts route are covered you will have to retrace the path to the main road, adding 2 miles (3.2 km) onto the walk. If in doubt about the river level it is best to return via Huccaby Cottage.

Having made the decision, cross the bridge and follow the main road up the hill. The road can be busy so it is important to keep well in to the side. Follow the grass verge (L) through the gate by the cattlegrid.

This is the parting of the ways. If taking the principal route (to miss the stepping stones) continue along the grass verge (L), passing Hexworthy Cross, then Huccaby Cottage. The path L18 starts at the gate beyond the cottage (please shut the gate securely). Follow the wall (R) through Huccaby Tor Newtake to the gate at the corner of Snider Park Plantation. Secure the gate and continue uphill in the direction indicated by the signpost and after a few yards you will cross a dry leat.

This leat brought water from the Cherry Brook (west of here) to the tinworkings at Brimpts. There was mining activity here for about 10 years from 1797 and again from 1849-55. Several good quality lodes were worked but the money was lacking at crucial times in the development of the mine.

From the leat an indistinct grassy path continues up the hill through Brimpts Newtake. **From the high ground there is a panoramic view.** The southern edge of Bellever Forest will come into view straight ahead; our route goes through the gate you can see in the wall of the forest. Immediately ahead the ground drops steeply into a little valley, the head of Winford Brook. The path crosses the valley, skirting the boggy area, and on the far side joins the wide track L28 near the gate. The Forestry Commission especially request that people do not smoke in the plantations because of fire hazard.

Enter the plantation and continue downhill along the forest track (L18), passing another track (L). Continue along the track (L18) which runs straight ahead, following signposts, to Bellever. Emerging from the Forest, at the metalled road turn left, then fork right over the cattle grid. **The houses at Bellever were built in 1947 to accommodate the forestry workers.** Follow the road nearly to the brow of the hill to a point where a rough track (R) leaves the road. From here our route (L18) is a grassy path on the contour at a slight angle (R) of the road. At first it is not clear but soon it becomes obvious as it gradually bears away from the road. Nearing Postbridge the path steeply descends between gorse bushes to a hunting gate. Follow the wall (L) to the road and turn left to the car park.

Alternative route to be used if the stepping stones are passable:-

If taking the route to the stepping stones, turn right onto the track L26 at the Forestry Commission sign. Beyond the small cattlegrid, at the immediate division of tracks, L26 is the right-hand fork. A conifer plantation was first established at Brimpts in 1862. Following the 1914-18 war the Prince of Wales conceived a scheme to plant 5,000 acres (1195 hectares) of moor with the newly introduced Sitka spruce of which just over 3,000 acres (1214 hectares) was actually planted. This, it was hoped, would help replenish the nation's timber resources and provide jobs for the unemployed. Brimpts was extensively planted in 1921. The Forestry Commission bought the plantations in 1930 and continued planting until 1935.

At the next junction go straight ahead to Brimpts. If you have a dog slip it on the lead as the path goes straight through the yard and there may be stock or farm dogs loose. Brimpts was originally a settlement of 3 ancient tenements and was first mentioned in 1307 as 'Bremstonte'.

Pass the back of the farmhouse and continue straight across the yard to the field gate beside the cottage (L). Beyond the gate turn right along the edge of the field to another gate in a wire fence just below. Then turn (L) away from the buildings through another gate onto a wide track. Make sure all gates are secured behind you.

At Brake Plantation (L) continue across the field to a gate near the East Dart River. Cross the next field and at the far gateway the path passes in front of a ruined cottage. At the beginning of the 19th century a local man brought his newly-wedded wife to this remote spot to place her out of reach of her ardent admirers. Dolly, and Dolly's Cot as the building is called, gained a certain local notoriety.

Enter Brimpts Northern Wood through the little gate and follow the path up river until the Walla Brook joins the East Dart River from the north. The stepping stones are just above the confluence.

WARNING: if the stones are impassable then the route must be retraced past Brimpts farm to the main road. (Turn to page 15, paragraph 10). There is NO right of way along the riverbank up river.

Cross the stones and walk up the west bank of the Walla Brook to the clapper bridge on that brook. Cross the bridge then continue up the east bank bearing right, away from the stream, to the road. At the road turn left and walk to the entrance gate to Babeny Farm.[4] The ruined building (R) by the gate was a corn mill built c.1303 by the holders of the ancient tenements at their own cost, the timber being supplied by the king from his woods. The right hand gatepost is said to be a bearing stone from the mill.

If you have a dog it should be on a lead as the path again passes straight through the farmyard. Climb towards Babeny Farm on L25 and take the rough track (R). The path double bends upwards leaving the house and newer barns (L) and the older buildings (R). Babeny was originally 3 ancient tenements and the probable positions can still be made out by the two groups of buildings (R) and the modern house (L) which stands on the site of the third. The wide area in between (where the path goes) is known as 'The Run' and was used to turn stock out during the winter. You are still likely to encounter a cow or pony as well as farmyard fowl and dogs.

Continue along the track from the farm. Where the track narrows and bends right, look over the wall (L) across the valley to the two newtakes, Blackator (L) and Winford (R). The area near the wall where they meet lies in ridge and furrow showing early cultivation (possibly several hundred years old).

The gate at the end of the lane opens onto Riddon Ridge. The path can be followed by keeping near the wall (L) all the way to the stepping stones at

Stepping stones, Laughter Hole　　　　　　　　　　　　　　　　　　17

Laughter Hole. Laughter Tor is across the valley, just south of the Bellever Plantations.

Approaching the East Dart River, go through the hunting gate beside the plantation and cross the stepping stones at Windford. This area is known as Laughter Hole. The name 'Laughter' comes from Lough Tor, so Laughter Tor has the word "tor" repeated! 'Hole' is applied to a stretch of narrow river valley. From the stones follow the waymarked path between the wall (L) and the fence (R). The stream you cross is the Winford Brook. Enter Bellever Forest through the gate. The Forestry Commission especially requests that people do not smoke in the plantations because of fire hazard.

Follow the ride with the wall (R) until you reach another, wider ride where you turn right. These rides allow machinery into the depths of the plantations. Bellever Forest is planted mainly with Sitka spruce which is thinned after 25 years of growth and every subsequent six years. This obviously causes some disturbance and the Forestry Commission takes special care to keep the paths open. The thinnings are used for paper-making and fencing.

The ride joins with two tracks – a forestry track (R) and L18 from Huccaby (L). Join L18, passing below Laughter Hole Farm (L), thereafter straight ahead to Bellever. In the Forest are some examples of Contorta Pine (R). These were planted amongst the Sitka two or three years after the first planting to replace failures. Another name for this tree is lodge pole pine – American Indians use the central pole in their wigwams or lodges.

For the rest of the walk see above, beginning 'Emerging from the Forest ..."
(p. 16 para 3).

MAP
PAGES
72, 74

BELLEVER FOREST

Bellever Forest covers some 1356 acres (549 hectares) and is owned by the Forestry Commission. There are three car parks within the Forest from which two walking routes are waymarked, one shorter route marked with yellow topped posts and a longer one with red topped posts. Rights of Way also pass through the forest linked with paths provided by the Commission. Access is permitted on the open moorland of Lakehead Hill and around Bellever Tor. Taken together, the area offers many walking opportunities. A map board in the main car park outlines the paths, and this map is printed as a leaflet for sale in the Postbridge Information Centre.

There is a pleasant picnic area on the west bank of the East Dart River below Bellever clapper bridge. Toilets are nearby in the main car park.

Bellever Forest.

Prehistoric cist and retaining circle, Lakehead Hill.

DUNNABRIDGE

Dunnabridge is on the main road, equidistant from Two Bridges and Dartmeet. It lies within the area known as Dartmoor Forest. The 'Forest' is the central part of Dartmoor and does not refer to the number of trees, but signifies past ownership and use by the Crown. In about the 9th century, sometime after the Saxons settled, an area of the moors became a hunting ground for the kings. This was formally made a royal Forest following the Norman Conquest, and the kings imposed the strict forest laws to preserve the deer, boar, wolf and hare which they hunted. In 1204 King John disafforested Devon and peripheral parts of Dartmoor. 35 years later the Forest of Dartmoor was granted to the Earl of Cornwall, heir to the throne. To this day it forms part of the estates of the Duchy of Cornwall.

The valleys of the East Dart and the West Dart Rivers within the Forest were colonised in the 13th century. It is possible to identify 17 different sites containing 35 farms, now known as the ancient tenements, but several unidentifiable names remain in early records. The tenements were copyhold (also known as customary freehold); the evidence of title was in the rolls of the manor court and a copy was held by the tenant (or copyholder). At a change of ownership (by inheritance or sale) the land was surrendered to the Lord of the Manor who admitted the new tenant as named by the former tenant. This was simply a legal formality, the only interest of the Lord of the Manor being that he received a payment, for example, the best beast on the farm, from the former tenant on surrender of the land.

The holders of the tenements had certain customary privileges; they could pasture sheep and cattle in the Forest, without payment, cut peat for fuel and take stone for building. Until 1796 they could also enclose 8 acres (3.2 ha) of land, a newtake, from the Forest. But there were also certain customary services to perform; until the mid-19th century they had to assist at the drifts of stock from the Forest, and there were courts to attend at Lydford Castle.

The following walk passes near or through the sites of 5 groups of these tenements.

MAP PAGE 74

DUNNABRIDGE – SHERBERTON – HEXWORTHY, return via HUCCABY – HUCCABY TOR

5¼ miles (8.5 km), about 3½ hours. WARNING: there are STEPPING STONES over the West Dart River between Dunnabridge and Sherberton and also just below Sherberton. If the stones are impassable then the path must be retraced to Dunnabridge. For information on rivers and stepping stones see page 5. A walk through the farmland of some of the ancient tenements. Paths used: L27, L20, L28.
Start the walk from the metalled car park just west of Dunnabridge, beyond the double bend; it is not signed from the road.

Turn right, downhill, along the road verge and continue with caution, across the road bridge over Dunnabridge Water. The track (R) is the entrance to Dunnabridge Farm and the buildings (L) are Dunnabridge Pound Farm. (The track (L) across the grass to the road is the return route L28). Dunnabridge (now one farm) was once a settlement of ancient tenements and was first recorded as "Donnebrugge" in accounts dated 1305 when five tenants (thought to be the founders) held lands there.

Dunnabridge Pound is beside the road (L) just beyond Dunnabridge Pound Farm and is thought to also have an early origin. The tenants of all the ancient tenements had to assist at drifts when the cattle (three times a year) and the ponies (once a year) were driven from the Forest to the Pound. The tenants pastured the stock here for 2 or 3 days and any strays (those not entitled to be in the Forest) were then driven to Lydford to be claimed or sold. The tenants received a ½d loaf a day for attendance but could be find a noble (6s. 8d.) for non-attendance.

In the field below the main road the ruined farmstead walls of Brownberry can be seen. This replaced the original ancient tenement further down the hillside. This walk passes through Brownberry's fields, now part of Sherberton.

Dunnabridge Pound

Brownberry, West Dart Valley

Stepping stones across the West Dart at Swincombe Meet. In wet winter months these stones are usually covered.

Continue along the road; at first there are stone walls at the roadside on both sides but soon it is possible to walk on the verge (R). The stone wall (R) turns sharply from the road. The bridleway L27 can be followed downhill, beside the wall, and enters the fields through the gate at the bend in the wall below. It is important to close the gate securely so that the animals cannot stray onto the road.

Cross the corner of this field to the gate opposite and then follow the wall (R) through the next two fields. Looking up river, on the left bank, you may notice a small, modern building which belongs to South West Water. At this spot the height and velocity of the river are measured and recorded throughout the year. After heavy rain (which on the hills can fall in any season) the river may rise several feet in just an hour. Valuable advance warnings of possible flooding further downstream can now be given.

You are now beside the river. Turn to the left and walk downstream along the river bank. The river is running from the north and turns sharply left ahead. On this bend, where the river widens, the path continues across the stepping stones.

WARNING. If the stepping stones are impassible then the path must retraced to Dunnabridge. There is NO public right of way along the river-bank down river.

Continue in the same direction, now beside the River Swincombe (R). The path crosses the Swincombe at the stepping stones immediately below Sherberton Farm. These stones are small and may be covered by water but as the current is not strong in summer it would be safe to cross.

Sherberton also is an ancient tenement. It was first recorded in 1307 when there were three tenements called 'Sherborne', or 'lying in Sherborne'. As with a number of these tenements the house has been built comparatively recently but one of the old houses still stands, now serving as a farm building. Follow the path a few paces up river to the metalled road near the bridge. Turn left over the bridge and pass Wydemeet (L). Follow the metalled road up the hill to Hexworthy.

There was early tin streaming in the Swincombe Valley (R) and beside the road you can see the opencast working along the tin lode. In the 19th century, shafts were sunk here at Gobbet Mine (as it was then called). Dartmoor United Tin Mines, 1836-40, sank a shaft of 240 feet (73m), and Dartmoor Consols, from 1840, worked an adit of 900 feet (274m) on a lode. Two water wheels drove a pump to drain the workings and stamps to crush the ore. Plans for expansion were discussed in 1874 but little more is known of the mine.

The small, fenced building (beyond the opencast workings) is one end of a tunnel through the hillside to Hexworthy. It was built to carry the pipe taking water from the River Swincombe to Venford Reservoir as described in the walk from Dartmeet to Venford.

At the top of the hill you pass some of the houses of modern Hexworthy (L). Turn left at the road junction, downhill past the Forest Inn. Hexworthy was originally a settlement of three ancient tenements. Wheal Gobbet and other tin mines close by once provided enough trade for two pubs in this area. William Crossing stayed frequently at the Forest Inn (a much smaller and altogether different establishment from the present one) and Richard Cleave, the landlord then, often featured in his articles. In the years that Crossing knew Hexworthy he saw 23 "a few ancient thatched dwellings" disappear; of the modern houses he said "an incongruous feature in the shape of red brick has been introduced where only granite ought to be".[6]

The cross on the Green (R) was erected in October 1897 to commemorate the Diamond Jubilee of Queen Victoria. It was made at the quarry at Merrivale.

The little cottage built into the hill on the next corner is Jolly Lane Cot, reputed to be the last house built in a day on Dartmoor. This refers to the old practice of erecting a house and enclosing a piece of land in a single day between sunrise and sunset, the builder then claiming it for his own. When erected in 1835 by the Satterley family it was but a single storey and thatched; in 1901 a first floor was added and in 1976 the extension was built on at the back.[7]

Recross the West Dart River at Huccaby Bridge (also known as Hexworthy Bridge). Locally, occasions are recalled when the river has risen so high that it has crossed the road making it impassable. Huccaby House (R) was originally built as a fishing box, the summer residence of C. F. Burnard, and became the home of Robert Burnard, a leading antiquarian of his time and a founder member of the Devonshire Association and of the Dartmoor Exploration Committee which recorded and examined the prehistoric remains on Dartmoor.

The road continues past Huccaby Farm, once a settlement of four ancient tenements, and now one farm. At Hexworthy Cross turn left along the main road, which is straight here, and traffic therefore travels fast. At first it is best to walk on the stretch of grass (L) but passing Huccaby Cottage there are stone walls close to the road and walkers should go in single file.

The start of path L20 is at a 5-bar gate beyond the cottage. Again, it is important to check that this gate is securely latched. Bear left along the grassy path straight up the hill past Huccaby Tor. This area of enclosed farm land is known as Huccaby Tor Newtake and is maintained by Huccaby Farm as grazing for their stock.

When about halfway up the hill the path goes through Huccaby Ring. This is believed to have been a pound for enclosing stock, probably from prehistoric times. The remains of the wall can be traced from the stones still visible and from the gorse bushes which grow on the site. The name 'Ring' has been given to other similar enclosures.

Looking back along the path, Combestone Tor can be seen below the skyline (Holne Ridge). Then to the right is Down Ridge with the Forest Inn in front, the Swincombe valley and the mast at North Hessary Tor with Princetown in front.

Beyond the tor the path bends a little to the right, i.e. more northerly and passes over a stile into Brimpts Newtake. Comparing the two faces of this wall, the northern face is much the smoother. This means that Huccaby Tor Newtake is enclosed against stock from Brimpts Newtake. It also means that, by tradition, Huccaby Farm maintains the wall (although later sales and leases can change this). Maintaining stone walls is costly for farmers both in time and money; to rebuild a fallen section can be a serious burden.

From the stile the path heads for the standing stone which you may notice near the skyline between Bellever Tor (L) and Laughter Tor. Shortly the path crosses a dry leat and looking to the left there is a cart-bridge spanning it. This leat ran from the Cherrybrook, west of Dunnabridge, to Brimpts, bringing water to the waterwheels of the tin-workings there.

The path follows the higher edge of Outer Huccaby Ring. **This is similar to Huccaby Ring but much bigger.** Beyond the Ring the path, narrow but well defined, follows the contour in the same direction and the standing stone is now clearly seen ahead.

The path climbs, passing some fenced tin workings (please keep OUTSIDE the fence), and reaches L28, a hard track.

The mine shafts are a part of the extensive Brimpts sett; at one time they were known as North Mine. This was at its most active in the 1850s and a shaft was sunk 26 fathoms (156 feet – 47.5m) into a good tin lode. Turn left along L28. The track runs downhill through Brimmeads Newtake and then through Dunnabridge Newtake. It is important to keep the gates of these two newtakes closed to avoid stock straying, as each belongs to a different farmer.

The track ends beside Dunnabridge Pound (L) and the main road is just below. Turn right for the car park.

DARTMEET

The River Dart and its tributaries drain a major area of the moors. East Dart Head (the source of a river on the moors is referred to as the "head") is a short distance from Cranmere Pool, and West Dart Head is a couple of miles south, between Cut Hill and Rough Tor. Both are within the blanket bog of northern Dartmoor.

These two rivers leave the high moorland near Postbridge and Two Bridges, respectively, and flow through the farmland of the ancient tenements. Here at Dartmeet, the East Dart flows past Badger's Holt to unite with the West Dart just beyond the bridge. Then as the Double Dart, the river flows down a deep, wooded valley past New Bridge and Holne Bridge to Buckfastleigh where it leaves the National Park.

The meeting of these rivers at Dartmeet is historically significant, as they form part of the boundary of Dartmoor Forest. The Norman kings reserved areas, known as Forests, for hunting, and special laws were applied. This boundary was in existence during the reign of Henry I (1100-1135) but later kings held the whole of Devon as a Forest. In 1204 King John stated that he would disafforest Devon up to the former boundary, and in 1240 a perambulation was made of the boundary by twelve knights. The two rivers were then referred to as 'Derta' and 'aliam Derta' (another Dart). They are 'Easter and Wester Dart' in 1609, and Dartmeet, as 'Dartameet', does not appear until 1616.

Nowadays, Dartmeet is a popular spot with the visitor, both for its pleasant situation and the licenced restaurant and tearooms, called Badger's Holt. There is a large private car park managed by the owners of Badger's Holt for their patrons and the general public.

Dartmeet Clapper Bridge

5 miles (8 km), about 3¼ hours. WARNING: there are STEPPING STONES at Dartmeet and at Week Ford. For information on rivers and stepping stones see page 5. A walk through farmland and moorland looking at farming methods (including reaves – prehistoric field boundaries) and also at water supply. A steady, but not steep climb to the reservoir. Paths used: H10, L40, L38.

From Dartmeet car park walk to the main road and cross the bridge. The river flowing past the car park is the East Dart River. Its confluence with the West Dart can be seen below the bridge. The path H10 (L) begins shortly over the bridge; it passes beside two houses and through a field gate. (The path L38 crossing the field is the return route of this walk). Walk (L) down to the river – the West Dart – and cross the stepping stones.

WARNING: if the stones are impassable, then this walk should not be attempted. The stones at Week Ford, which are smaller, will also be impassable. There is NO right of way along the river bank.

H10 continues in the same direction beyond the stepping stones and soon begins to climb between the oak trees (waymarked). Pass through the gateway into the fields and climb, following the hedge and wall (L). Approaching the next gateway you pass a sheep creep (L). This is a hole built in the wall to give passage to sheep between two fields while other stock are enclosed in one. This is necessary as sheep kept in a confined space for more than a couple of days will try to break out. There is usually a stone nearby to block the hole (missing here). Combestone Farm and Combestone Tor (pronounced "Cumston") can be seen ahead.

Drawing level with the farm, turn left through the gate. Ahead the path (H10) can be seen climbing the hill. The little stream crossed at the gate is domestic drinking water brought by leat from the O (Wo) Brook, 1 mile (1.6 km) distant. The small ruined building (L) formerly was used as a vag house. The vags (turves) cut on the moors in the summer were stored in the house to keep them dry ready for burning in the hearth. The track passes the house and buildings (L) and continues between the fields to a gate onto the moorland. It is sometimes known as Aller Brook Lane (named after the alder trees growing along the banks of the brook), or the Holne Track.

Many hazel bushes have been planted against the walls. Poles would be cut at regular intervals for jobs such as hurdle making and spars for thatching where small diameter wood is required. There are oak woods in the area which gave valuable oak bark for tanning leather.

The wall (L) at Combestone Wood is constructed of large blocks of granite which have been dressed (cut) and the gaps between filled with small rocks. The other walls are the more common rough dry stone walling. As the gate comes into 27 sight there is a good view of the River Dart in the gorge with Mel Tor (L) and Bench Tor (R).

At the gate the track continues over Holne Moor and can be clearly seen; in places it is slightly sunken. Passing through the gate you can see that the wall face on the farm side is uneven, but the face on the moorland side is smooth. This is to stop sheep, in particular, breaking in to eat valuable grass laid up for hay. Please shut the gate securely.

If you look beside the track (L) you can see that another track joins on; the lower edge is faced with stone. Buried beneath it is the pipe which brings water from the River Swincombe to augment the supply to Venford Reservoir.

As the track approaches the Aller Brook the remains of a small clapper bridge can be seen; nowadays the stream is forded below this bridge, but formerly the ford was above and the track (H10) continues from there. When well clear of the stream the track swings sharp right and climbs the hill. It is sunken here and rough where winter storm water has washed away the surface. Shortly after the bend, you pass a prehistoric hut circle (L), very close to the track but this can be partly obscured by bracken. Halfway up the hill the track crosses Holne Moor leat and shortly after the dry channel of Wheal Emma leat.

Aller Brook Lane (H10) ends at the metalled road from Holne. On a clear day there is a distant view ahead to the sea at Torbay and it may be possible to see on the skyline the spire of Priory Church and the tower of the parish church, both at St. Mary Church, Torquay. There is also an extensive moorland view looking from north to east (left to right). Combestone Tor is behind you and the large hill (R) is Holne Ridge on the edge of the high south moor.

The walk continues to the reservoir by turning left along the road; the left-hand verge has a good grass path. Holne Moor leat is met again beside the road at the place where it disappears underground. The water is piped across the dam and re-appears on the other side by force of gravity. Before the reservoir was built, the leat flowed along the hillside.

There are a number of rectangular stones beside the road to the reservoir (there is one at the end of the dam). They mark the edge of the catchment area of the reservoir. 'PUDC' stands for Paignton Urban District Council which owned the land inside the boundary and built the reservoir. 'H' is for Holne, the parish, and "RD' is Richard Dawson, the (then) Lord of the Manor, who owned Holne Moor.

Paignton Waterworks, as the reservoir and treatment works were then called, were opened in 1907 to supply that town. The reservoir was the second to be built on high Dartmoor and the water was much needed as Paignton was becoming a popular seaside resort. Just above the dam, amongst the trees, is the meter house and spillway where the water from the Swincombe enters the reservoir (the pipe track was seen after Combestone Farm). The supply of water draining from Holne Moor along the Venford (Wennaford) Brook was found to be inadequate so in 1926 work began on laying the pipe from Swincombe. The water is shut off when the reservoir is full or when there is not enough water in the Swincombe for extraction.

The return walk is made by retracing your steps to the brow of the hill and continuing past Aller Brook Lane to Combestone Tor, the pile of rocks straight ahead by the road. Grass verges are on both sides of the road most of the way.

Compare these two sides of the same wall; on the outer moorland side the face is smooth to prevent sheep and cattle from breaking into the enclosure.   29

Pass the 'PUDC' stones then look to the skyline (L) between Holne Ridge and the tor; you may be able to see a tall stone. This is Horn's Cross which marks the ancient trackway from Holne Moor to Walkhampton Common and probably linked Buckfast and Buckland Abbeys, (an alternative to the Abbot's Way).[8]

On the bend before climbing to the tor you pass various gullies and spoilheaps made by tin mining. Since the early 19th century this spot has been known as Hangman's Pit. A farmer returning from Brent Fair where he had exchanged his pony for another which he found to be inferior, was so upset that he hanged himself from a tree here.

You soon reach Combestone Tor at 1156 ft. (352m) and Dartmeet can be seen below at 750 ft. (228m) above sea level.

Notice that across the Dart Valley on the hill opposite there are at least a dozen parallel lines, though in summer the sun may be too high and bright to see them. These are prehistoric (2nd millenium BC) land boundaries known as reaves and take the form of low, vegetation-covered walls similar in appearance to those of the more familiar prehistoric hut circles and enclosures. Cross boundaries can also be made out. The reaves continue on this side of the moor; indeed one runs directly between the natural granite outcrops of the tor here.

Turning round, and looking to the south-west, a conspicuous wall can be seen running roughly along the contour. Above the wall is open moorland. Running downslope from it can be seen traces of numerous parallel boundaries. This contour wall is in fact built on the line of the prehistoric Venford Reave which is at least 4½ miles (7.2 km) long, and much of which forms the southern terminal of the Dartmeet parallel reave system. This system extends for nearly 4 miles (6.4 km) and is 2½ – 3 miles (4-5 km) wide.[9]

From early in the 19th century various writers correctly identified reaves. However, as peat-cutters tended to find these reaves below ground level, there was also a school of thought which identified them as trackways and dated them as post-prehistoric.[10] Interest in reaves waned during this century until the last decade when they were again classified as prehistoric.[11] This led, in 1975, to the founding of the Dartmoor Reave Project with Andrew Fleming of the Department of Prehistory and Archaeology, University of Sheffield, as the Director. Some reaves have been identified by searching for references in earlier literature on Dartmoor and others have been discovered by studying aerial photographs and by fieldwork. It is often advantageous to view the moorland in winter when a light covering of snow drifting against the banks makes them particularly obvious. Survey work on Dartmoor has been carried out under the Project and it is now felt that the basic pattern of the reaves is understood. It is considered that Dartmoor was divided into a number of territories each based on a river valley and organised by a single community. The system of reaves was probably partly used for cultivation while the upper moorland served as common grazing land shared between the groups.[12]

Continue down Combestone Hill to Saddle Bridge spanning the O Brook. The whole length of the O Brook has been streamed for tin across the valley bottom. On the right bank especially, the cliff can be seen which marks the edge of the worked ground. Also, upstream and just out of sight are the more recent Henroost and Hooten Wheals mines which were still in production this century.

Prehistoric reaves in the Dart Valley.

The ruined building beside the bridge contained a Pelton Wheel which supplied electricity to the mines in later days.

WARNING: If the stepping stones at Dartmeet were only just passable, then do not continue to Week Ford as these stones will certainly be covered. Cross Saddle Bridge and follow the road through Hexworthy and over the river via Huccaby Bridge. The route can be rejoined at L38 opposite Huccaby Farm (see the last three paragraphs of this walk).

Otherwise, at the O Brook turn right before Saddle Bridge, pass a gate (R) and climb the stile in the fence. This fenced area along the bank of the O Brook, is owned by Devon County Council and access is permitted as far as the confluence of the brook with the West Dart River. The path is uneven due to tin streaming. At first follow near the fence (R) but soon a way can be found beside the stream. Near the end of this path you pass a solitary gatepost where the remains of a wall coming from the right meets the stream. The path goes through this wall and continues over another ruinous wall and then continues by the fence (R).

The footbridge was built by the National Park Rangers with help from the Army. This bridge is often covered by water during winter storms. Cross the footbridge and follow the bank of the West Dart River to the stepping stones which you cross.

WARNING: If the stones are impassable then the path must be retraced to Saddle Bridge. Follow the directions already given from there. There is NO right of way along the river bank.

The return route now follows an ancient track from south west Dartmoor to the Widecombe district which is a branch of the track mentioned near Venford. The path passes over land belonging to Huccaby Farm where South Devon cattle are bred. Dogs must be kept on a lead from now until you reach the car park. 31

Week Ford Lane, L40, passes between blackthorn bushes and climbs the hill with stone walls on both sides. As you reach the top the lane widens and is used as a field, which may be muddy nearer the buildings. Hexworthy can be seen to the left; the large white building is the Forest Inn. The farms here kept many South Devon cows before the war and it was a common sight for the roads to be busy with ponies and traps taking cream and butter to market.

At the end of the lane continue in the same direction, passing the buildings and silage pit (R). Enter the waymarked field gate (the start of footpath L38) and walk straight ahead up the field; a sign is soon visible ahead. The path runs by the wall (R) and drops steeply between gorse bushes. Turn right through the gateway and follow the track straight down the hill.

There is a good view of the reaves (seen earlier from Combestone Tor) on the hill ahead.

The path continues over the modern stile. Go through the next gateway (L) and cross the field to the gate by the bottom (grey) house. This is where the walk started. Return over the road bridge to the car park.

MAP
PAGE
74, 75

DARTMEET – COMBESTONE TOR, return via WEEK FORD – HUCCABY

2¾ miles (4.4 km), about 1¾ hours. WARNING: there are STEPPING STONES at Dartmeet and at Week Ford. For information on rivers and stepping stones see page 5. A walk mainly through farmland. A long, steady climb to Combestone Tor which has much-photographed views. Paths used: H10, H17, H13, L40, L38.

From the Dartmeet car park walk to the main road and cross the bridge. The river here is the East Dart; Dartmeet is just down river. The path begins soon after (L) and passes beside two houses and through a field gate. (The path L38 crossing the field is the return route of this walk). Walk (L) down to the river – the West Dart – and cross the stepping stones.

WARNING If these stones are impassable you should not attempt the walk. At this point there is no alternative path. The stones at Week Ford, which are smaller, will also be impassable. There is NO right of way along the river bank.

Once over the stepping stones, the path H10 leaves the river and crosses a flat field. This was the bed of the river at the end of the last Ice Age, about 10,000 years ago, when a river, much larger than the present Dart, poured down from the hills. Rounded granite boulders carried down by the torrent can be seen on the ground (R). Climb the waymarked path between the oak trees. Pass through the gateway into the fields and climb following the hedge and wall (L). Combestone Tor and Combestone Farm can be seen ahead; locally the name is always pronounced (and sometimes spelt) "Cumston".

Drawing level with the farm continue to climb now following the metalled track H17. Approaching the gate onto Holne Moor you pass a number of holes; these are believed to be early opencast tin-workings. Beyond the gate the track, now H13, continues to climb. Cross Holne Moor leat and later the dry channel of Wheal Emma leat.

Holne Moor leat brings water from the O (Wo) Brook, over Holne Moor, to supplement the Holy Brook which runs below Holne village. As the brook nears Buckfast the extra water is taken out, by leat again, to Higher Buckfast Mill where it is used. Locally, the leat is also known as Hamlyn's leat (from the days when the building was a woollen mill owned by Hamlyn Bros.) or Buckfast Plating Company leat. The leat dates from about 1800 or before, when the woollen mill started. It is vital that any leat carrying water should never be blocked or diverted as people's jobs or drinking water for people and livestock may be endangered.

Wheal Emma leat was constructed in 1859 and brought water from the River Swincombe to the River Mardle which flowed past Wheal Emma Mine, a copper mine near Buckfastleigh, where the water was used to power the operations. From the Swincombe the leat crossed the O Brook by a wooden launder, then ran parallel with Holne Moor leat and, skirting the head of the Holy Brook, dropped steeply to the River Mardle. The copper mining industry had declined by the end of the 19th century and the leat went out of use. The length of Wheal Emma leat from the River Swincombe to the River Mardle is over 9 miles (14.5 km).

Leats – man-made watercourses – are numerous on Dartmoor and were constructed to lead water, from take-off points on a stream or river, for all its many purposes.

The track H13 ends at the metalled road; Combestone Tor is just above. The return walk is as the previous walk; down Combestone Hill to Saddle Bridge (R). There is a choice of either descending at once to Saddle Bridge (turn to page 31 from paragraph 2) or first visiting Combestone Tor.

The Dart Valley.

MAP
PAGE
75

EASTERN COOMBE (near DARTMEET) – YAR TOR – CATOR GATE, return via CORNDON

4 miles, (6.4 km), about 2¾ hours. A walk zigzagging between tors crowned with cairns which mark prehistoric burial sites, and over a landscape patterned with ancient field boundaries. Marvellous views on a clear day.

From the car park at the top of Dartmeet Hill where the road bends before descending to Dartmeet, cross the main road. Climb straight to Yar Tor 1,360 feet (414m). There is an extensive view from Yar Tor, especially to the north where the conifer trees of Fernworthy can be seen on the skyline, and to the west to Princetown with its Prison, and the radio mast on North Hessary Tor. The East Dart River flows down the valley below Yar Tor to join the West Dart at Dartmeet. A cairn on the tor has been re-built in modern times to form a circular shelter.

Leaving Yar Tor, head north of east down towards the little road leading to Sherril and Rogue's Roost. At this metalled road turn left to Hornet's Castle and Sherril. The ancient spelling of Sherril was 'Sherwell' which has now been re-adopted, although the pronunciation remains as "Sherell". On the far hillside above the road to Sherril a distinct pattern of prehistoric parallel reaves and small rectangular fields can be seen. A signposted track (W26) leading to Cator Gate leaves the road just behind Hornet's Castle (R). Climb the hill using this track and beyond the field walls continue straight to Cator Gate (no gate exists today). (Option – You can make a pleasant detour by dropping down to the Walla Brook below, where there is a crossing place known as Vennyford. Do not cross, but notice on the opposite bank the gate across the ancient driftway which divides the fields of Babeny (L) and Riddon (R). This barrier stops the straying of animals between the Forest of Dartmoor and Spitchwick Common, and is one of the very few man-made features on the Forest Boundary. Continue upstream with first the Walla Brook on your left and then the farm walls of Riddon, to the rough track leading from the farm. Turn right along this track to the metalled road near Cator Gate).

At the junction with the road at Cator Gate, look almost due south (R) and you will notice a grassy bank running straight up the hill to the long Corndon ridge. Follow this bank and when it ends continue straight up the hill. After about ¼ mile (0.4 km), the gradient will decrease. Continue along the ridge, curving gently to the left and heading straight for the two large heaps of stone (marked tumuli on the map). These prehistoric artifical mounds are raised on the sites of one or more interment(s). These are magnificent examples in terms of size and position.

Continue to Corndon Tor where there are two more cairns. The main road and car park lie to the south-west. Turn down the hill in that direction using the well worn path which passes the memorial cross. Recross the minor road, and 50 yards (46 m) further on look for a ring of stones which form the surrounding circle of a kistvaen (prehistoric stone chest). The kistvaen would have contained a burial. Two of the four slabs forming the chest are still in place and the large, flat, covering slab has been pushed to one side. The cairn circle marks the mound of earth which once covered the kistvaen. The remains of a much robbed double stone row leads from the cist and can be traced for a considerable distance. Bear left around the worst of the bracken and head for the car park.

COMBESTONE TOR – HORN'S CROSS – O BROOK, return via leat

MAP PAGE 75

3½ miles (5.6 km), about 2 hours. A moorland walk needing good visibility but with gentle gradients and easy to follow. Wet underfoot. Horn's Cross is one of the markers and a point of interest. Also see and follow some of the many leats in this area and explore the fascinating mining remains in the O Brook valley.

Combestone Tor.

From the car park area at Combestone Tor cross the road and follow the wide grassy track in a southerly direction.

Turn left for a few paces along the terminal reave of the Dart Valley reave system and right through the gap. From here you can see a stone cross standing in the dip ahead; walk directly to it. Known as Horn's Cross, it stands on an ancient track running between the Abbeys of Buckfast and Buckland. The route from Buckfast was via the crossroads 'Stumpy Oak' (where a cross has been re-erected) and Play Cross in Holne village. On Holne Moor, the track crossed the little Venford Brook and continued to this cross. Horn's Cross and a cross to the west on Down Ridge guided the traveller to Horse Ford between the two where it was possible to cross the O Brook. The path marked by crosses continued westwards over Ter Hill to Nun's Cross then on to Walkhampton Common, leaving the moorland near the 19th century Burrator Reservoir.

50 paces or so further on from the cross you encounter an old leat channel. Turn right along it until you reach a large gulley. This gulley was created by extensive tin streaming in medieval and Elizabethan times. Notice that the leat was constructed on top of the waste heaps confirming that although it was also built by miners (to take water from the O Brook to gulley workings further along) it was built after the workings you are now crossing.

Continue past the gulley still following the leat (now a reed-filled channel) until reaching the valley of Drylake (lake here meaning a stream). This stream marks part of the boundary between the Commons of Devon and the Forest of

The north north east view from Combestone Tor.

Horn's Cross

Dartmoor (owned by the Duchy of Cornwall). The perambulation in 1240 of this boundary refers to Drylake as 'la Dryeworke' showing that the valley was being worked for tin over 700 years ago.

Still following the leat, the waste tips of a mine rear up ahead. Cross both branches of the next stream (a little upstream of the leat channel) and ascend the slope of the lowest tip where the circular concrete dressing floors of Hexworthy mine open out before you. Hexworthy Mine was a late 19th and early 20th century development of earlier tin mines (Hensroost and Hooten Wheals) in this upper area of the O Brook. Little is known of the earlier mines, but from the 1880s to 1919 Hexworthy was worked under a series of different leases with high outputs in certain years. The two circular buddles that you see here at the lowest part of the dressing floor were where the heavy tin ore was separated from the lighter sand or gravel after it had been crushed. An armature fixed at the middle swept around the buddle, washing the sandy waste to the edge.

About 45 men were employed here in the year 1908. As was traditional with Dartmoor miners, many had to walk long distances from their homes to work an 8 hour shift. In fact the majority would remain on site for the whole week. From the bottom of the dressing floor continue in the same direction as previously following the track which passes a fenced-off wheelpit (R) and runs on to a clapper bridge over the O Brook. From this bridge it is possible to continue upstream to the Hensroost workings, returning the same way. Otherwise cross the O Brook and continue along the same track.

On the left is a ruin which was once the mine captain's house, office and the barracks for the workers. Along with many of the other mining structures in this area, it was largely destroyed by American troops during the Second World War. Bullet marks can still be seen on the walls.

Just after this ruin turn right downhill on another wide mine track. Immediately ahead on the skyline can be seen the Down Ridge Cross. Where the track peters out you will see a stone faced embankment (L) and a fenced area (R). The embankment once fed water from a leat to a wooden launder high in the air to a waterwheel in the now fenced-off pit. This massive wheel, 45ft (13.7 m) high, powered all the pumping, crushing and separating machinery. It became redundant in 1907 when a water turbine (Pelton wheel) was installed at Saddle Bridge on the O Brook giving 140 hp.

The wheel disappeared in the 1930s and in 1980 the wheelpit was shored up and made good by the National Park Authority as an impressive example of its kind.

From the lower end of the wheelpit bear slightly right down to the river and find a place to cross just above the confluence with the stream from the Dry Lake gulley opposite. Turn left and walk downstream by the O Brook.

Where the river bends left the line of three leats can be seen on the hillside ahead. The lowest is the Holne Moor leat and still supplies water to farms near Holne. The middle leat supplied water to Combestone Farm and the highest took water to the River Mardle for use lower down by a copper mine called Wheal Emma.

Follow the highest of the three leats to the road. Turn right uphill, and back to the car park by Combestone Tor.

This is the site of a deserted medieval settlement known today as Hutholes. Within about one acre (0.4 hectare) lie the remains of six buildings dating to the 13th and 14th centures AD. In the 1960s the owner, Mr Herman French, drew Hutholes to the attention of Mrs Minter who was then excavating similar ruins at Houndtor. Consequently archaeological excavations under her direction were carried out. Mrs Minter concluded from her work that before the stone structures visible today were built, the site was occupied by a number of turf walled houses recognisable by the holes left in the ground by wooden supporting stakes. Each turf house had been rebuilt many times which suggested a long occupation beginning perhaps as far back as the 8th century AD.

Hutholes is the subject of a Management Agreement between the National Park Authority and the late Mr French who generously made the area available for the public to enjoy. So there is now public access to the land within the fence. People wishing to visit the site by car must park by the road on Dunstone Down (see top right of map page 75) and walk down the road towards Dockwell. Hutholes is in the second field on the right. Visitors are asked to avoid damaging the archaeological remains by not jumping or climbing on walls, to respect the wildlife, leave no litter and to shut gates.

This is a promontory overlooking the Dart valley at a particularly spectacular point. From the small parking area at Cold East Cross, Buckland Beacon is only about 1 mile (1.6 km) away over relatively dry moorland. Inscribed on the outcrop are the Ten Commandments and other sacred passages. This unlikely and painstaking work of craftmanship, now suffering from the effects of weathering, was the brainchild of Mr. Whitley, Lord of Buckland Manor in the 1920s. Upon hearing that Parliament had rejected a proposed revision of the Book of Common Prayer, Mr. Whitley celebrated this defeat by having these granite blocks inscribed in situ.

NEW BRIDGE

New Bridge, spanning the River Dart, is on the main road about 4 miles (6.4 km) from Ashburton. The River Dart is the parish boundary between Widecombe and Holne. New Bridge was formerly Holne New Bridge and Holne Bridge (between New Bridge and Ashburton) was Holne Old Bridge. Both bridges date from the early 15th century; New Bridge appears to have been a completely new bridge and Holne Bridge was rebuilt after it was destroyed by a flood in 1413. The Bishop of Exeter, Bishop Stafford, granted certain indulgences to all those who helped rebuild it. It is likely that the original bridge was of timber as were a number of others rebuilt with stone in the 15th century.

The approach to New Bridge on the Ashburton side used to be narrower and there was a gate across the road by the bridge. This was a moorgate, kept shut to stop the stock straying, and is now replaced by a cattlegrid. During the last war, to stop heavy military vehicles from damaging New Bridge, a Bailey bridge (built of wooden planks and steel girders and named after the British inventor, Bailey) was slung across the river just up stream. After the war the road to the east was widened when the wall was rebuilt.

The visitor to New Bridge will find a car park and public conveniences. During Easter to October a National Park Information Centre is open daily.

New Bridge

2½ miles (4 km), about 1¾ hours. The scenery is outstanding: the wooded Dart near New Bridge, the panoramic views of the Dart Gorge and the high tors beyond. The climb to Holne is steep but refreshments await at the pub and tearooms. Paths used: H9, H11.

From the car park cross New Bridge and turn right through a small lay-by over a stile onto path H9 through the trees of Cleave Wood. The National Trust owns this stretch of woodland along the river.

The path runs close to the River Dart, which along this stretch has several small waterfalls. The rock forming most of Dartmoor is granite but here on the edge there is slate; this is the rock that forms the bars across the river. If the river is low, you can also see granite boulders which have a speckled appearance against the single colour of the slate. These granite boulders, some of them quite large, are several miles from the parent granite mass, having been washed down in the flood waters of the Dart at the end of the last Ice Age. The path bends away from the river and divides; go left uphill. (The path (R) continues near the river through the National Trust woodland).

Emerging from the woodland into a field, continue along the track. Turn left where signposted over the stile by a gate in the top hedge. The track you have just left is an entrance to Holne Cott which was a hunting box attached to Holne Chase, the hunting seat of Sir Bourchier Wrey, Lord of the Manor in the last century. There is a good view from the stile back along Cleave Wood to Leigh Tor below the skyline and (L) to Holne Wood. Climb steeply, bearing right up the hill to the stile in the field corner. This field overlooks Holne Village – birthplace of Charles Kingsley – on R. Continue in the same direction up the next field and then follow the path to the road.

At the road turn left. (To see Holne village take the next turning right at Butts Cross.) Once around the corner the road climbs and there is a wide grass verge (R). Bear right at the next junction for Gallant le Bower. The seat at the fork in the road commemorates the Coronation of Queen Elizabeth II. There is a good view from here, or over the gate opposite, of the Dart Valley and neighbouring moors.

Take the right-hand fork to Gallant le Bower. The name Gallant le Bower (or Gallantry Bower) is found elsewhere in England; it has been suggested that they were secluded spots suitable for lovers' meetings.

From Gallant le Bower turn left rather steeply downhill. At the next junction notice a direction stone (L). The stone has been shaped; on one face a raised 'A' for Ashburton has been cut and on another a 'B' (for South Brent) and on one of the narrower sides is a 'T' for Tavistock. It is one of three similar stones between Ashburton and South Brent believed to date from the second half of the 17th century.

Walk on down the road and just beyond Chase Gate Farm turn left by the wood. The path H11 passes between hedges to a stile. From here there is a good view of Hannaford Manor (a private house) designed by architect Sir Edwin Lutyens and built in 1904-11 from Cornish and local granite.

The path follows the hedge (R) through two fields to a stile in the bottom right hand corner. At the main road turn left, taking great care on the bend. You soon reach the car park at New Bridge.

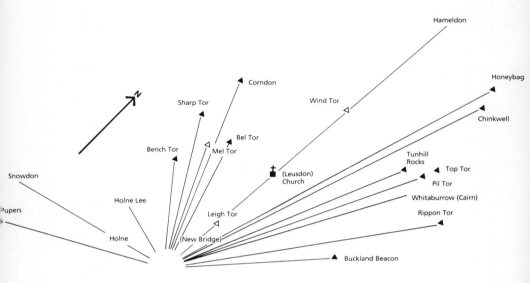

MAP
PAGE
76

NEW BRIDGE – MEL TOR, return via PONSWORTHY – LEUSDON – DEEPER MARSH

7½ MILES (12 km), about 5 hours. A moorland walk along Dr Blackall's Drive giving spectacular views of the wooded Dart Valley, takes you up to Sharp Tor before descending along lanes to the attractive village of Ponsworthy. Back to Newbridge via footpaths through fields and woods. It is not recommended on a day of poor visibility.

Take the minor road which leads from New Bridge upstream past the car park. Follow this road up the hill, passing through the hamlet of Hannaford. On reaching the open moorland continue along the road as far as the rough track leading to the old quarry (L). Turn left on to this track and shortly turn right, up the hill, following the wide grass path. This leads directly to Dr Blackall's Drive, a wide track which contours the hillside high above the River Dart. Dr Blackall of Exeter bought Spitchwick Manor in September 1867 and occupied, as a summer residence, the mansion erected by John Dunning, the first Lord Ashburton, nearly 100 years previously. When his wife became unable to walk on Dartmoor, Dr Blackall had the track constructed to take a pony and trap so that she could still enjoy the moorland.

Turn left onto this track and before reaching above the old quarry, turn right uphill following a wide grassy path for about 1 mile (1.6 km) until Mel Tor appears straight ahead. The track turns sharp right past Mel Tor and continues between the fields as Mel Tor Lane. Several gateposts along this lane have slots cut in them from the days when wooden posts were slotted across the opening rather than the swinging gate of today. The posts have all been turned from their original position, facing across the gate, and now face outwards.

Beyond the lane, the track divides. Follow the wall (L) to the minor metalled road. Turn left along the road until you cross the little stream, Simon's Lake. 25 yards (8 m) beyond the stream bear right uphill on a grassy path to the summit of Sharp Tor.

From the top of Sharp Tor follow the gently sloping grass path northwards towards a stone wall and fields. Keeping the wall on your right follow the path to the road junction. Here take the road, marked Sherril (L), passing Ollsbroom Cross (R) which for years was used as a gatepost at Lower Town until it was re-erected in its original position in a rather damaged state.

Continue along the road, keeping straight on at the next two junctions. The road descends steeply down to Ponsworthy passing between some pollarded trees. At the bottom of the hill you come to a ford called Ponsworthy Splash. A short detour for refreshments could be made here by turning left over the bridge to the village Post Office and stores.

Notice the stone incorporated into the bridge and inscribed 1666 and 1911. In 1664 it was recorded that 'Ponsworthy Bridge, in Withycombe, near the foot of the Mor' was in a state of decay and £30 was needed for its repair. The dates on the stone indicate the years of the repairs. From Ponsworthy Splash turn right up the hill. Around a double bend the wooded valley of the West Webburn River with Buckland Beacon framed behind come into view. On reaching the next road junction fork left, keeping straight on at the next junction. The road takes you steeply downhill past Leusdon Church (L) and Leusdon Lodge (R) to Lower Town. Just past the slate fronted house and barn turn right along a small footpath. Passing through a gate carry on through two fields, keeping the hedge on your right, to a hunting gate in the corner. Go through the gate, and follow the hedge (R) to another hunting gate next to a metal field gate at the metalled road.

Turn left down the road until it turns sharply right, past the houses. Here turn left over a stile. Pass through three fields following the hedge (L). In the third field the track bears left downhill, over a stile, and enters a wood with a stream on your left. At the end of the track carry straight on through a double metal gate to the road. Continue downhill on the road, turning right at the bottom. The road follows the Double Dart (the East and West Dart Rivers combined), past Spitchwick Lodge (R), where the river itself bends sharp R at Lower Corner Pool. Here, turn left off the road and continue upstream along the riverbank.

The River Dart at Deeper Marsh, Spitchwick. The river embankment on the right was rebuilt in 1977, by the Dartmoor National Park Authority, using large boulders to repair damage caused by heavy recreational use.

Notice the steep outcrops of rock on the far side of the river where the force of the river has undercut the riverbank. On the near side, the river is banked with large boulders and netting to hold the vegetation and soil together. This work was done by the National Park Authority to prevent further erosion of the riverbank from the pressure of visitors using the area.

The path climbs high above the river and bears left where it nears the road. Continue by the river and back to the car park after passing under Newbridge.

VENFORD RESERVOIR

In 1900 Paignton Urban District Council obtained powers to construct a dam across the Venford Brook, having realised that the contours of the valley would be very suitable for a reservoir. The dam (completed in 1907) was built of Dartmoor granite and carries the Holne to Hexworthy road. The reservoir holds 198 million gallons and serves the Paignton and Brixham area. Below the dam are the treatment works where up to 2 million gallons of water per day are filtered and chlorinated. In the late 1970s the Dartmoor National Park Authority built toilet facilities and two car parks to cater for the numbers of people attracted by the beauty of this small area of clear, still water in an unspoilt landscape.

Venford Reservoir.

VENFORD RESERVOIR – HOLNE WOODS and return

MAP
PAGE
75

1¾ miles (2.8 km), about 1 hour. Short walk through moorland and woodland starting from the car park beside the public toilets near to the dam.

From the bottom of the car park on the western side of Venford Reservoir head north, away from the road, on a path through the bracken veering slightly away from the iron fencing surrounding the South West Water treatment works.

45

Sharp Tor, from above Holne Woods.

Enclosed within the fence are the Superintendent's house, being part of the original construction, the filtration beds (within the tin sheds) and the chlorine house which was a later addition. The plantation consists of mostly larch and spruce with a few Scots Pine.

Past the end of the plantation the view opens to the north-east looking across to Bench Tor. Standing at 1,060 feet (323 m) (550 feet (168 m) above the River Dart) it is always spoken of locally as Benjie Tor. The path follows the contour above the valley of the Wennaford Brook until the first views open down into the valley of the Dart. In the river as it bends around the promontory are the boulders known as the Broad Stones. At certain times the sound of the water hurrying through this spot is borne on the breeze; this is called the 'cry' of the river and is said to herald bad weather. Looking ahead across the river you may see Rowbrook House below the pyramid-shaped Sharp Tor and away to the right Mel Tor.

Veer left keeping to the same contour on to a path leading to the pipe line track which carries water from the Swincombe intake to the reservoir. Looking across the valley as you follow the track you can see the Dart flowing past Luckey Tor and Rowbrook Farm. It was from this farm that Jan Coo, a young boy employed to tend cattle, was lured to the river, and to his death, one night. Some believe that it was a Dartmoor pixy calling his name and others that it was proof of the rhyme – 'River of Dart, Oh, River of Dart, Every year thou claimest a heart'.

The track now enters the wood and passes along above the very steep valley slopes on which grows a mixture of oak and birch trees with occasional thorns, sallow and beech. Part way along you will pass a small fenced area which is part of the regeneration trials being carried out by the Dartmoor National Park Authority which owns this stretch of woodland. Except for a few beech saplings below Bench Tor there is a total absence of young trees and hence no regeneration of these woodlands. Uninfluenced, it seems that in the long term the valley side will become gradually denuded of trees as the present trees age and die. The establishment of younger trees is prevented mainly by grazing stock which have access to these woods, although oak seedlings also have difficulty in growing under the shade of their own species.

Follow the track along out into the open again where to the west can be seen Combestone Tor. As you proceed you will also see views of Brimpts forestry plantation and up the River Dart to Dartmeet. The track becomes less discernible but walk slightly downhill keeping above the wood until you come to a small tributary of the river. You soon come to a ford and the remains of an old clapper bridge where Allerbrook Lane (Bridlepath H10) crosses the stream.

Turn left and follow the slightly sunken track uphill and back towards the reservoir. Travelling up the hill you will pass a large hut circle on your left and then Holne Moor Leat which still carries water to Buckfastleigh. Looking back the eye can follow the leat running round the edge of the hill on which Combestone Tor stands. Two hundred yards (62 m) further on you cross the dry channel of the Wheal Emma Leat before coming to the top of the track beside the road. Turn left and follow the road back to the car park.

HOLNE

Holne is a small village on the edge of the moor. The parish extends to the summit of Ryders Hill, 1,691 feet (515 m) above sea level (the highest point on southern Dartmoor), where there is a bound stone known as Petre's Bound Stone. The parish is bounded on one side by the River Dart from Dartmeet. The village of Holne is described in the following walk.[13]

The manor of Holne (the village and surrounding farms, and much of the woodland and moorland) is said not to have changed hands by purchase from 1066 until 1885. The Domesday Book (1086) records that William de Falaise held several manors including "Holle" (Holne), "Estoche" (the Stoke farms above the Dart), "Dertrintone" (Dartington, near Totnes). William did not appoint a steward but himself held the demesne (home farm) at Holne and Dartington. The two manors remained together until the 14th century when Joan Martin (married to Nicholas de Audeley) inherited Holne.

The Audeleys already held Tawstock (North Devon) and, together with Holne, the estate passed by marriage to the Bourchiers, Lords Fitzwarren and later Earls of Bath, then in the 17th century to the Wreys. Holne Chase (near the Dart) became the hunting seat of the Bourchier Wreys. In 1885 the manor was sold by Sir Bourchier Park Wrey, Bart. to the Hon. Richard Dawson, the first time that the Manor of Holne had been sold.

The new Lord of the Manor and his son both died in 1914. In 1926 most of the outlying farms were sold by auction. Following Mrs Dawson's death in 1932 the manor was split up with many of the former tenants buying their own cottages and farms.

A popular attraction in the parish of Holne is the River Dart Country Park near New Bridge, 1 mile (1.6 km) from Ashburton and situated on the River Dart. The parkland, lakes and the various facilities, such as the adventure playground, are open to the day visitor.

MAP PAGE **78**

HOLNE VILLAGE

1¼ miles (2 km), about ¾ hour. A short walk around the village by lanes and footpath. Path used: H5.

From the car park in the centre of the village turn right. The building (R) was the village school until 1946 when it closed with only 8 pupils, following the transfer of the senior pupils to Buckfastleigh some time previously. It is now the Village Hall. The Church House Inn (L) is believed to date from 1329. The oldest part of the village is in the sheltered hollow around the crossroads. Above are Village Farm and Stares Nest, the Church and the Church House Inn. Village Cottages are the slate-hung terrace, locally referred to as Tinners' Cottages. Sparrows Hall (once thatched) is opposite and below is Holne Court Farm. Holne Court was once the manor house but in the late 18th century it became fashionable for the lord of the manor to build a mansion in parkland away from the village and Holne Court became just a farm.

Go straight ahead at the crossroads and up the hill to the next junction, Butts Cross. You pass the new vicarage (R), built in 1975. Butts Cross takes its name from the adjacent field. Most villages have a 'butts'. The name dates from an Act of 1466 stipulating that every village should erect archery butts and that each man should practice on them every feast day, or pay the penalty of a half-penny. The range of the long bow was 300-400 yards (275-365m), the bow was roughly 6 ft. long and the arrow 3 ft.

From Butts a detour can be made (R) up the hill to the Coronation seat for a panoramic view of the moors and the Dart valley. Otherwise turn left and follow the road for Hexworthy. A leat runs beside the road for some distance. It is one branch of Holne Town Leat which brings water from Holne Moor over 2 miles (3.2 km) to the village. It is still in use and is regularly maintained by the villagers.

At the cross-roads keep straight ahead. Further on you pass a tithe barn. During the Civil War (1642-6) the West Country experienced much fighting. At first Devon was under parliamentarian control. Locally, the Lord of the Manor of Holne was Henry Bourchier, 5th Earl of Bath, and a leading royalist. In the Commission of Array issued by the King on 19th July 1642 he was ordered to organise, arm and train the country's militia for the purposes of defence against the enemies of the kingdom. This he energetically undertook from Tawstock Court, his property in North Devon. On 28th September he was arrested by order

The Church of St. Mary the Virgin, Holne.

49

50   Holne Church: memorial window to Charles Kingsley.

of Parliament and the royalists for a while lost all direction, but by the end of 1643 they had swept victoriously through the county under impetus from Cornwall.

Following the parliamentarian victory in the Midlands in 1645 the New Model Army, commanded by Sir Thomas Fairfax with Oliver Cromwell as lieutenant general of horse, with disciplined and regularly paid men, marched into Devon. The conditions that winter were very bad; the men were dying of the plague and of exposure due to the very wet weather. The royalists meanwhile were recruiting men with difficulty as they were rarely paid, (there being little money), and the militia were essentially local forces not used to being far from home and were prone to desertion.

On Friday, 9th January 1646, a detachment of foot and horse from Cromwell's army crept into Bovey Tracey after dark and surprised the royalist officers while they were playing cards. The army advanced to Ashburton the following day but the royalists had already abandoned the town, reports of the defeat at Bovey having been carried by the men fleeing in panic. Cromwell's men, no doubt aware of Holne's royalist Lord of the Manor, plundered the tithe barn belonging to the vicar and fed their horses on his corn.

By the 13th January the royalists had been chased across the Tamar to Cornwall; the strongly parliamentarian Plymouth was released from its two year siege and the royalist Exeter surrendered. Fairfax marched on to Oxford.

By the barn is the entrace to the Glebe. It was in an earlier house on this site that Charles Kingsley was born while his father held the living here for a short time.

Turn left at Vicarage Cross. The seat here commemorates the Silver Jubilee of Queen Elizabeth II. The first field (R) is known as the Glebe lands. Take the second gate (R) onto the footpath H5, shutting the gate securely behind you. Alternatively, you can return along the road, passing Michelcombe Lane (R).

The footpath crosses another branch of the leat. Follow the hedge (L), go over the stile and follow the fence (L). There is a good view of Scorriton (below) and the hills of Pupers and Snowdon (R). Snowdon was called thus as long ago as the 13th century and today is badly hit by snow storms, often being much whiter than the surrounding hills. A gert (a large opencast tinworking) known as Gibby's Beam runs across Snowdon. The hollow seen at the end of the gert is Snowdon Hole. At the end of the path go over the stile and turn left along the road from Michelcombe.

At the end of Michelcombe Lane the gate opposite (L) is the entrance to the field, Play Park, used by the villagers for festivities. The Holne Revel (a Ram Roasting Feat) was held here every Midsummer's Day until the late 19th century. In addition to dancing and merrymaking the revel also featured wrestling, at which Holne men were reputed to be most skilled, and pony racing over the surrounding hills. Village people still come to Play Park for events such as Bonfire Night.

From Michelcombe Lane turn right for the village and left at the next junction which is called Play Cross. This may have been the site of an ancient cross as it is on the line of a track across the moors which is thought to have linked Buckfast and Buckland Abbeys.

Return to the car park.

5½ miles (8.9 km), about 3¾ hours. A woodland, farmland and moorland walk with several steep hills. Paths used: BW4, BW14, BW15, BW2.

From the car park at Holne turn left through the village. At Play Cross turn downhill (L) for Scorriton, keeping on the metalled road and passing Littlecombe (L). At the bottom of Littlecombe Hill go left over Holy Brook Bridge. This stream has only been known as the Holy Brook in recent times. It flows into the Dart a short distance north of Buckfast Abbey and its first recorded name was the Northbrooke. It appears in a charter, believed to date from 1148 or soon after, as a boundary of a parcel of land given to the Abbey by Roger de Nonant from an adjoining estate.

Scorriton is soon reached. The first building (L) is the Methodist Chapel dated 1904 with a series of foundation stones bearing the names of local benefactors. Continue straight through the hamlet, passing (L) the Tradesman's Arms and Scorriton Farm. (The lane (R) at the Square is the return route.) Pass Rosemary Lane (L) and when clear of the village turn right for Coombe (waymarked LWR HR Coombe).

At the bottom of the steep hill cross the River Mardle at Coombe Bridge and take the road (R) to Higher Coombe. The houses of Coombe are spread along the banks of the Mardle for nearly ½ mile (0.8 km). The modernised house (R), 'Old Chimney', was a mining house with a high chimney stack which could be seen for miles around. It was taken down long ago for safety reasons. Straight ahead is Mardlewood House. The front of the building was modernised this century but the back, seen shortly from the footpath, still shows the stone work and small-paned windows.

At the end of the metalled road bear left at the Great Oak and walk around the side of the houses. The grass track BW4 can be seen leading to the woodland.

The track climbs steeply through the dense Scae Wood. Beyond the stile at the top of the wood the track then continues in the same direction with oak trees first on (R), later on both sides, then on R again. If you have a dog with you it is wise to put it on a lead as there may be sheep in the fields but out of sight until you are nearly upon them. In recent years with modern machinery it has been possible to improve this ground by ploughing and reseeding. Beyond the trees, there is a view back to Holne and further on is the house in the valley, Warmmacombe, (R).

Crossing a stile at the end of the oak trees, contour right across the field to another stile. Continue with the silver birch trees (R) to the corner of the field then steeply uphill (L) keeping the hedge (R). Go through the hunting gate in the corner of the field, turn left over a small leat and then through the large metal gates, turning right into BW14. At the end of the lane you reach Lud (Lyd) Gate opening onto Buckfastleigh Moor.

The gate was anciently called 'Lyd Yeat' and was one of the old moorgates in the boundary between the enclosed land and the moorland. Beyond the gate the moorland has been formed into a stroll (a space between two enclosures). This area is ideal for stock to shelter in during bad weather. Notice the very large gorse bushes beyond, which also give shelter. The stroll can also be used by farmers for sorting their stock, as at the pony drifts (late September-October) when the moor ponies are rounded up.

From Lud Gate bear right along the path BW15 to the corner of the field (R) and go straight downhill following the wall (R). You may notice that on the moorland side of the wall there is a large ditch, known as a cornditch. These ditches date from when Dartmoor was a royal hunting-ground of the Norman kings. The Forest Law stated that no landowner could stop the king's deer with a fence or a hedge from regaining the Forest. The cornditch, with a ditch and vertical stone wall on the moorland side backed by a wide sloping ditch on the other side, made it difficult for a deer to jump into the enclosed land but if one did it could easily step out again. The name cornditch originates from the cornlands that they protected (corn was widely grown on Dartmoor farms then). Nowadays the ditch is not maintained and a wall has had to be built on the bank.

As the hill steepens the wall bears right and the path continues straight ahead. A stream can be heard running by the wall and there is another on your left. Ford the left-hand stream at the head of a steep gulley and as the River Mardle comes into view bear right, down to Chalk Ford down a wide grassy track. At the ford there is also a footbridge which you cross. In the river just above the bridge there is a stone with the carving "1815 IG".

The track BW2 passes through the gate and follows the hedge (L). The view (R) is of Scae and Lakemoor Woods. Go through the next gateway and the track then slowly descends between the fields to Scorriton. It is in a good state of repair as it was reinstated after the Second World War: you may notice some inscriptions (GPOW 1946) set in the cement storm gulleys.

Approaching Scorriton, the first farm, Higher Town, (L), has an upping stock against the end wall which was used to mount a horse. Until the moorland roads were improved in the last century everyone travelled on horseback. A farmer could not usually afford a second horse for his wife so on the occasions when she went away from her home she rode pillion on a cushion behind her husband.

At the Square in Scorriton you can turn left and return to Holne along the outward route; otherwise turn right at the Square then left by the telephone box. At the next junction turn left and cross the Holy Brook. Take the rough track (L) straight up the hill. This is often referred to as Langaford Steep and is the most direct road to Holne but has not been used frequently since the days of horses and carriages; these were always directed along more circuitous routes to miss the hill. At the top, rejoining the metalled road, continue straight ahead to Play Cross and the village (R).

BUCKFAST AND BUCKFASTLEIGH

The original settlement was near the River Dart at Buckfast where a Benedictine Abbey was founded and endowed by King Canute in 1018. In 1148 the Abbey became a Cistercian monastery and remained so until the Dissolution in 1539. The Cistercians were traditionally great traders; the monks of Buckfast dealt particularly in wool, and their consignments would have crossed the moors by such tracks as the Abbots Way. In 1539 the deed of surrender was signed, the lands were distributed and the buildings were dismantled. Three and a half centuries later in 1882, Benedictine monks, exiled from France, acquired the land and rebuilt the Abbey to the original plan. The stone used is local grey limestone and the golden sandstone of Ham Hill, Somerset.[14]

Buckfastleigh, 'the clearing of Buckfast', probably originated in the 13th century. It developed in two parts, called Higher and Lower Town, and lay close to the River Mardle and the Dean Burn, making full use of their waters for washing wool and, at a later date, powering machinery. Buckfastleigh, with the rest of the country, suffered the loss of trade due to wars in Europe at the turn of the 18th century, particularly the Napoleonic Wars, which effectively closed overseas markets for years at a time. As a result of these wars, and the competitive trade in this country from finer quality fabrics and machine produced material from the North, the industry failed in many Devon towns. The East India Company maintained the smaller scale industry for almost another 50 years by buying Devonshire serges and selling them at a loss in the Chinese market. This

Buckfast Abbey from near Buckfastleigh Parish Church.

monopoly was broken in 1833 but Buckfastleigh somehow survived and in 1838 was operating 700 of the 3,000 serge looms in the county. At the turn of the century there were four mills processing the wool by fellmongering and combing, and producing blankets and serge. The industry continues today in Buckfast and Buckfastleigh.

Parish boundaries had an ecclesiastical origin but in 1894 an Act of Parliament caused some to be changed when civil parishes were formed for administrative reasons. Buckfastleigh was split into Buckfastleigh (the town area) and Buckfastleigh West (the rural area) which extends about 4 miles (6.4 km) to Buckfastleigh Moor where the boundary is marked by bound stones. One, Petre's Bound Stone, stands at the summit of Ryders Hill, the highest point on southern Dartmoor. William Petre was a clerk to Henry VIII and his signature appears on many deeds of surrender including that of Buckfast Abbey. Following the Dissolution, Petre was able to buy the Buckfast estate of the former Abbey which included Buckfastleigh Moor.

Included in Buckfastleigh West are two hamlets, Scorriton and Coombe, lying at the edge of the moor. The houses of Coombe are situated along the steep-sided Mardle valley and, in the past, cottage industries made full use of the abundant water supply. Scorriton lies on a ridge of higher ground and has grown in size more recently.

In the town there are car parks off Plymouth Road, Station Road, and Chapel Street all close to Fore Street. At Buckfast there is a paying car park at the Abbey. Buckfast is fairly well served by bus services.

BUCKFASTLEIGH TOWN TRAIL[15]

MAP
PAGE
79

2 miles (3.2 km), about 1¼ hours. Along the narrow streets you can see many sturdy looking town houses, as well as old buildings and stores which remain as relics of the woollen industry. On the periphery of the town lie the homes of the 19th century mill owners, now converted to other uses. Path used B4.

Our walk begins in the car park behind the Globe Inn from which we turn left and then left again into Chapel Street. A feature to notice in Buckfastleigh is the large number of alleyways which lead to interesting buildings behind the main streets.

Buckfastleigh made full use of the River Mardle to power its mills. It is said that, in the 16th century, there were seven in existence in the town. The extensive factory site (R) was developed by Hamlyn's (a local family business) from 1846. In 1896, a limited company was formed and at the turn of the century Hamlyn's was the largest of four mills in the town. In 1920, the business was bought by the Co-operative Wholesale Society. The complex now supports a variety of small-scale industries.

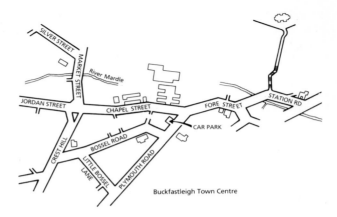

Buckfastleigh Town Centre

Continuing along Chapel Street, we find the Congregational Church (L). It was built in 1872 at a cost of £1,350. The Loosemore Centre has recently been established here as a workshop for the building of organs, and a centre for the study of early music. Across the road is the Methodist Chapel (R) with its large-scale early 19th century Doric porch.

Chapel Street leads up to Higher Town and what was the market square. A market was granted to the Abbot of Buckfast in 1352, but Buckfastleigh market never prospered because of the nearness of Ashburton.

Turn left into Bossel Road. Harewood House (L) is now converted into flats but was the administrative centre of Buckfastleigh Urban Council after 1950.

Shortly turn right down Little Bossel Lane. On the right is a recreation ground first provided by the Hamlyn family in 1921. A plaque relating to this event can be seen on one building.

Ahead Little Bossel Lane becomes an alleyway opening onto Plymouth Road. Turn left along Plymouth Road. On the right-hand side is Tollmarsh with its elaborate window brackets. Passing the car park (R), notice the leat (L) with bridges leading to the houses.

Turning left into Bossel Road brings us to the Town Hall and Library. Built in 1887 and enlarged in 1924, this building was also provided by the Hamlyn family, as the date stone on the northern side indicates. It is constructed of local limestone with Bath stone and brick facings. Walking back into Plymouth Road we are confronted by St. Lukes Church opposite. It was dedicated in 1894 and is of simple Victorian design with lancet windows. Prior to the building of this Chapel of Ease, a small school-room in the centre of town was used for evening services because the walk up to the Parish Church was too much for many of the elderly parishioners. Subsequently, the school-room became so overcrowded on Sunday evenings that it was proposed a Chapel be built, and a fund was set up to pay for it.

Plymouth Road leads into Fore Street. The pair of houses (Nos. 25 and 26) immediately before the Post Office (R) were probably built in the early 19th century. Notice the slightly bowed ground floor and windows.

Further down Fore Street are the ambitious stucco fronts of The Kings Arms and National Westminster Bank (R). Built in the early or mid-19th century, the building has large windows and moulded architraves. It was at the King's Arms that the quarry owners held their annual 'lime-feast', the occasion when the annual accounts between the farmers and quarry owners were settled. During the year the farmers from surrounding parishes would go to the quay at Totnes to load culm (coal) which they would then take to the limestone quarries. Here, in the beehive-shaped kilns, alternating layers of limestone and coal were burnt to produce the lime. The farmers returned home with lime which they spread on the fields to reduce the acidity of the moorland soil.

Opposite the end of Fore Street, at the corner of Station Road, is a late 18th century two-storey block (R) (both with contemporary door cases and panelled reveals). No. 13, Station Road (L) has an attractive, decorative frieze below the eaves.

Continue down Station Road, crossing the River Mardle which is joined here by Dean Burn (R). A few yards on (L) are the steps leading up to the Church of Holy Trinity. A little way up the steps there is a fine panorama of the whole town.

The steps (nearly 200 of them) leading up to Buckfastleigh Church.

The tower of the Church of Holy Trinity was built in the 13th century, the spire being a later addition. Near the south porch is the Tomb of Richard Cabell, enclosed in a metal-barred penthouse some time after his death in 1677. The reason for the penthouse was to quieten his spirit or, as the local people put it, "to keep him in". Cabell had an evil reputation and is said to have been so wicked that fiends and black dogs breathing fire raced across Dartmoor and howled around his tomb. Conan Doyle's 'Hound of the Baskervilles' may have been based on this legend.

At the east end of the Church is a ruined chapel of 13th century date. During the 13th century many Cisterican Abbeys built a small chapel known as 'The Chapel Without The Gate' for the use of the local people. It may be that the monks of Buckfast followed this practice and that this is their chapel.

From the east end of the churchyard, take the track downhill. Bear right and right again through a gateway (now onto footpath B4). The track passes through Higher Kiln Quarry, a limestone quarry which was in use until about 80 years ago. The modernised buildings (L) belong to the Pengelly Trust, the first caves study trust to be set up in the country. Several caves lead into the hillside from the quarry face and it was the discovery there of animal bones (mammoth for example) from an inter-glacial period which led to the Trust's foundation.

The Pengelly Trust has made detailed studies of the remains of invertebrates found in the caves, the formation of stalagmites and stalactites and the bat population. The organisation is run by volunteers, so the caves are only open to the public at certain times.[16]

You may also notice three limekilns (L) beside the track. These are just a few of those which were in operation in the district.

At the bottom of the hill turn right along the road back to Buckfastleigh. The A38 dual-carriageway can be seen just below (L) and beyond this is Buckfastleigh Railway Station, now the terminal of the Dart Valley Railway steam trains. The branch line, originally from Totnes to Ashburton, was built in 1872 and ran along 9½ miles (15.3 km) of broad gauge. The Great Western Railway took over from South Devon Railway in 1897 and nationalisation occurred in 1948. The passenger service ceased in 1958 and the line was closed in 1962. The Dart Valley Railway Company has operated the line to Buckfastleigh since 1969 (the A38 dual-carriageway has now been constructed over the line to Ashburton).

Turn right into Station Road. The Rock Hotel (R) was formerly a Preparatory School built in the early or mid-19th century.

Continuing along Station road, you again pass the steps to the Church and from here you retrace the outward route. Turn right into Fore Street and left into Plymouth Road to the car park (R).

BUCKFASTLEIGH – MERRYFIELD – HOCKMOOR – BURCHETTS WOOD – MILL LEAT – HAWSON CROSS – COOMBE – SCORRITON – HOLNE, return via GALLANT LE BOWER – SHUTTAFORD – HEMBURY BRIDGE

MAP
PAGE
78, 79

9 miles (14.5 km), about 6 hours. A walk along the valleys of the Mardle and Holy Brook to the moorland villages of Scorriton and Holne. Muddy patches after rain. There are pub refreshments at both villages and tearooms at Holne. Paths used: B5, B2, BW1, H7.

Find Fore Street and from its western end take Chapel Street which leads to Higher Town. To your right is the former CWS wool factory and across the road is a row of cottages from the earlier period when the processes of the woollen industry were carried out at home. The weather-boarded top storey was originally undivided along its length. It is here that the scoured (cleaned) wool was dried and combed although the row is known as the Weavers' Cottages.

Fellmongery is still practised; see the sign (R). It is the process of taking the hides of animals with the hair on (the fells) and curing the skins either with the hair still on (e.g. sheepskin rugs) or after removing the hair (e.g. leather, and wool for textiles).

At Higher Town continue straight ahead along Jordan Street towards Hapstead. The end of Higher Town is soon passed and the road continues through farmland to Merryfield (R). Merryfield Road is almost free of traffic as it ends at Hapstead House. Hapstead dates from the 15th century and was rebuilt by a member of the Hamlyn family who were the wollen manufacturers at Chapel Street from 1846 until CWS took over in 1920.

Buckfastleigh was well-known for the great abundance of superior quality cider. Apple trees remain at Merryfield and Wotton (L) but at many farms the orchards have been grubbed out.

Beyond Merryfield turn right (opposite the road to Wotton) onto footpath B5. Follow the track across the field, over the River Mardle and into Hillah Wood. The path bends to the left and climbs between the trees. It joins another path (B2 from Bilberryhill). Take the upper route which bends right and, beyond the wood, follows a lane.

At the metalled Oaklands Road turn left and at the next junction bear left to Hockmoor Head. Watch out for traffic (it is advisable to walk in single file). From the map it seems likely that the roads (L and R) were part of the Abbot's Way (Buckland Abbey via Cross Furzes to Buckfast Abbey). The road ahead was on an alternative 'Abbot's Way' via Holne.

From Hockmoor Head go straight on towards Holne (still in single file). The bridleway BW1 starts at the edge of Burchetts Wood (R) which is owned by the National Trust. Pass Burchetts Lodge (L) and continue along the track with woodland (L) and a field (R). The path then proceeds through the wood in the same direction, soon going downhill. The right-hand side is marked by a former

59

field bank. Turn left at the bottom passing a ruined barn (R) at the lower edge of the wood. Stay on the woodland path which becomes a sunken lane on entering Hawson Wood. About halfway along this walled section is a ruined cottage (L). The Retreat, as it was called, was a two storey, slate-roofed cottage with a small field opposite, which has become derelict since the last war.

Near the far end of the wood is another ruin (L). This was a corn mill until the end of the last century and was used by farmers wanting grain ground for livestock feed and for domestic flour. The mill was powered by water from the Holy Brook (R); the wheel pit can still be clearly seen. At the end of the track cross the Holy Brook and at the metalled road there is a choice of routes.

To shorten the walk by 1 mile (via footpath H7) turn right to Mill Leat and, passing the barn (L), take the first gate (L). Follow the footpath H7 along the hedge (L) through two fields to the metalled road. The last section is a steep climb (still by the hedge on your left). Turn left along the road (look out for traffic), passing Langaford (R), to rejoin the longer route at the rough lane by the orchard. (Turn to page 61 paragraph 4.)

Otherwise, to follow the full length of the walk (via roads) through Coombe, turn left. Take the road by the Holy Brook which then turns up the hill to Hawson Cross. At the junction turn left, then almost immediately right at Stumpy Oak. The old cross marks the ancient trackway which is believed to link Buckland Abbey with Buckfast Abbey. It runs from Walkhampton Common, past Fox Tor (south of Princetown) and across Holne Moor, to Holne. A number of rough granite crosses mark the way at such points as fords and crossroads and on the open moor. Compared to the Abbot's Way (the accepted route) it is more direct, (by one mile) and also has the advantage of crossing no major rivers. The cross was taken from a hedge and restored in 1952 to what is thought to be its original position.

The Stumpy Oak is a pollarded oak. The pollard is cut at 8-10 feet (2.4-3.0 m) leaving a permanent trunk, called the bolling, and the shoots grow from there. This method, rather than coppicing where the shoots grow from the ground, is used to protect the shoots from being eaten by animals (including the ones using the trackway). The poles would be cut regularly for firewood or for jobs about the farm. The trunk has started to decay with old age and no poles have been cut for many years.

Stumpy Oak.

Continue down the hill towards Cullaford Bridge spanning the Mardle, and turn sharp right by the cottage. This valley contains the hamlet of Coombe which stretches for ½ mile (0.8km) along the river. Beard's Farm (L) ('Beard's tenements' early in the 18th century) bears the name of a local family who are still well represented in the area. Further on, is the former village hall (R) (now a private residence) given in 1937 by the Lord of the Manor. It had ceased to be the school in 1934. The terrace of cottages next door was used by woolcombers; notice the weather-boarding on the end wall of the top storey. By the cottages there is a stairway where a pump still stands leading to the work area.

Woolcombing is a lengthy and arduous process whereby the wool fibres are teased out so that they are parallel, and drawn out into a loose continuous sliver ready for spinning. The job of the woolcomber was the last to be mechanised, but by 1850 the technique was perfected and within a few years no hand workers remained. White's Directory of 1851 records that there were 300 woolcombers in the Buckfastleigh district.[17]

Eighteenth century woolcombers.

At Coombe Bridge take the road (R) to Scorriton, up the hill beside the thatched cottages. At the top of the hill turn left to the village. If in need of refreshments continue through the village to the Tradesman's Arms; otherwise turn down right by the telephone box. At the next junction turn left and cross the Holy Brook into Holne parish.

Just before Langaford take the rough lane (L) up beside the orchard, to Holne. This is another stretch of the ancient trackway between the Abbeys of Buckfast and Tavistock. Continue along the metalled road to Play Cross, the site of one of the old crosses used to mark moorland tracks. Turning right through the village, pass Holne Church (L).

From the crossroads take the road towards Ashburton and turn right at the next junction, known as Butts Cross. Nearing the top of the hill fork right to Gallant Le Bower, about ½ a mile distant (0.8 km). There is a good view of the Dart Valley from this junction.

There also used to be a fine view from Gallant le Bower (indeed in later prehistoric times a look-out over the Dart was situated here) but it has been obscured entirely in recent times by an increase in the number of trees and bushes. The area and surrounding verges were used by several local farms as rough winter grazing when the weather conditions on Holne Moor were too harsh. Nowadays it is rare to see stock grazing here and natural regeneration of the trees has occurred.

From Gallant le Bower turn right and follow the metalled road around a sharp right-hand bend. It is best in this instance to walk in single file on the left-hand side of the road (on the outside of the bend). At the next junction, Humphrey's Cross, turn right, down Magpie Hill to Shuttaford.

Just before reaching the farm turn left down the green road, known as Lower Hembury road, which leads to Hembury Bridge. At first the lane runs between the fields of Shuttaford Farm and then passes into Hembury Woods, owned by the National Trust. Shortly afterwards you meet the Holy Brook again. Across the valley is Burchetts Wood which you passed through earlier. In 1978-9 the land from here to Hembury Bridge was improved by draining the meadows and by laying the hedges. Nowadays laid hedges are not often seen as mechanical trimmers are widely used.

Hembury Woods are mainly coppiced oak. Coppicing is done by felling the trees close to the ground and allowing several shoots to grow from the stump. These poles were harvested about once every 30 years; the bark was stripped and sold locally for tanning leather and the wood was made into charcoal. In this area copper rather than tin was mined and the main period of production was the latter half of the 19th century.

You may also notice the hills made by the wood ants. Several generations of ants work to collect the debris and construct the hill which is a waterproof shelter for the extensive chambers underground. Please do not disturb the hills.

At the metalled road turn right over Hembury Bridge. The next road junction is a staggered crossroads; go straight ahead onto the major road then turn right along Hembury Cock Hill (this spot is known as Fritz's Grave). At the top of the hill go left at Liney Cross; Buckfastleigh is soon in sight (R). At the crossroads, Round Cross, turn right (however, if the road is busy go straight across and take the next turning right, down Church Hill, as this will be more safe and pleasant). Return to Higher Town along Market Street and from there turn left down Chapel Street.

Overlooking the valley of the Dart is Hembury Castle, one of the many Iron Age hillforts on the edge of Dartmoor. It is a delightful site to explore, with well preserved ramparts and ditches. Its flat interior contains a surprise – a very small medieval castle which was probably built as part of the Norman Conquest and subjugation of this area. It has a motte and bailey earthwork which made use of the much older prehistoric ramparts as additional defences.

The Castle and surrounding woods are owned by the National Trust which has recently cleared the thick woodland scrub from the site. The Trust has also provided a small car park and picnic area south of the hillfort on the other side of the road. There are attractive woodland walks from here down through Hembury Woods to the River Dart below.

Hembury: motte and bailey earthwork.

ASHBURTON

Ashburton is about halfway between Exeter and Plymouth and lies just within the National Park on the borders of Dartmoor.

It has been suggested that from Saxon times Ashburton was a town of some importance. The still existing office of Portreeve is believed to have its origin in the 'port gerefa', the head of a Saxon market town, who was appointed by the king to witness transactions of property and goods, to assess the amounts of fines in criminal cases and administrate generally.[18]

Ashburton was part of the vast estates of the Bishops of Exeter from before the Norman Conquest until the early 17th century when, in the reign of James 1, it became the property of the crown and was later sold to laymen. The bishops had founded a market by 1155 and formed the borough of Ashburton before 1238.

In 1314, Bishop Stapledon granted his private chapel, dedicated to St. Lawrence, to the town. This was on the understanding that a chantry priest was appointed who would say prayers for his soul and all the Bishops of Exeter, past and future. This endowment was also used to benefit the town by providing services such as a water supply. The original document recording the acceptance of this gift still exists; attached to it is the impression of a seal of the arms of the Borough of Ashburton.

This seal shows the main influences on Ashburton's history. The building in the centre of the seal is thought by some to represent the Chapel of St. Lawrence, and by others the parish church which is dedicated to St. Andrew. A St. Andrew's Cross appears next to the building.

The alchemic signs of the sun and moon appearing in the seal represent the mining interests of the town. In 1305 a charter granted by Edward I named Ashburton as a coinage town, i.e. where tin metal produced in Devon could be assayed, taxed, then sold. The other coinage towns in Devon were Chagford, Tavistock and Plympton, the latter being added in 1328. Each town controlled a stannary (a tin mining district) and courts for each stannary were held in these respective towns. Originally coinages were held several times during the year but

Bishop Stapledon.

Arms of the Borough of Ashburton.

in the 15th century were usually held twice yearly. Each block of smelted tin was weighed and coined (a small piece was chiselled from the corner and assayed). The tin was then stamped and the dues paid according to its quality. This charter formalised Ashburton's position, as two years earlier over half of Devon's tin had been coined there and we know that for the previous 100 years large quantities of ore had been raised on Dartmoor. The industry had declined by 1600 but coinage continued on a small scale until the 19th century when the payment of dues was abolished by Act of Parliament.

The teazel seen on the seal represents the woollen industry which in the 13th century became established in towns throughout the county. It was especially the emblem of the fullers who, in the newly invented fulling mills, cleaned the woven cloth and raised the nap by drawing teazel heads across it. The industry declined with the spread of the Black Death and prosperity did not return until late in the 16th century when the technique of making a light worsted fabric was brought to this country by Flemish refugees. In 1672 a Tuesday yarn market was granted to Ashburton. The district specialised in combing and spinning the wool for worsteds but transactions took place at every stage of production – from the herdsman's fleece to the cloth bales of the merchant.

Although production was high it remained a cottage industry until 1817 when mechanisation of the spinning process was introduced to the town. The population in 1801 was 3,080 and due to increased labour required in the factories rose to 4,165 by 1831. But the end of industrial prosperity came rapidly when Devon lost its monopoly of shipping serges to China; by 1841 all work had stopped in the mills. The town's M.P., William Jardine, provided orders which gave employment during the next two years but despite this the industry collapsed.

Ashburton has a small museum at No. 1 West Street (in the centre of the town). It is open from mid-May until the end of September. For days and times of opening see the information board in the town car park. Admission is free. There are displays on tin mining and the wool trade: most striking is a pair of wool combs used in preparing the fleece for spinning into a worsted yarn. Visitors can also see a collection of prehistoric flint arrow-heads and implements, locally-made pewter, geological specimens (especially "Ashburton Marble"), a model of the old Market House demolished in 1848 and an internationally renowned North American Indian collection.

Ashburton Museum.

St. Lawrence Chapel (in St. Lawrence Lane) is also open on certain days from mid-May to the end of September (details on town information board and in the

Dartmoor National Park annual publication 'The Dartmoor Visitor'). From about 1546 (the date of the suppression of the chantry chapels by Henry VIII) a grammar school was established here until it closed for economic reasons on 22 July 1938. After this date the building was associated with the primary school but it was deemed surplus to educational requirements in 1983. The National Park Authority took on responsibility for the building. With a grant from English Heritage, some £110,000 has been spent on restoring the Chapel – in particular the very fine mid-18th century plasterwork. The building itself is well worth a visit and it contains an exhibition relating the fascinating story of the Chapel and the town. The recently revived Guild of St. Lawrence manages the Chapel and opens it to the public.

There are four main streets in Ashburton – East, North and West Streets and St. Lawrence Lane meet in the centre of the town. The town car park is best entered from North Street. The town is served by a frequent bus service.

66   St. Lawrence Chapel.

1 mile (1.6 km), about ¾ hour. A short walk around the ancient stannary town of Ashburton.

Leave the car park over Kings Bridge. The left-hand arch is the haunt of Cutty Dyer, a sprite once used to frighten naughty children. The slates on the slate-hung houses backing on to the river, came from a local underground quarry.

Turn left into North Street by the Italianate Town Hall, a building of local limestone and Haytor granite. In 1850 it replaced a wooden market hall. Over the portico are Lord Clinton's arms and, below, massive granite paving stones. Continue up the street, noting the dates above Pollard's Bakery. The former United Reformed Church is one of the country's oldest Nonconformist foundations, (1665). Unfortunately, the interior was gutted for conversion to commercial use.

Turn right into and along Stapledon Lane. The cottage chimneys still have the original slate flashings formerly used to prevent rain running down inside the thatch. The stone used is mostly local limestone and green volcanic ash.

Turn left into East Street. The many interesting houses include Number 31 with ornamental slating. Despite rendered frontages the massive chimneys and thick walls tell of 17th and 18th century construction, as do the fine proportions and deep eaves. Opposite the Golden Lion is the Conduit, a public water supply of 1797 restored by the Devon Historic Buildings Trust. There were three supplies of pure water provided by benefactors to the town. The house behind was the Spread Eagle, one of the many Coaching Inns which flourished here in the 17th and 18th centuries. Roborough Lane was the main road to Exeter.

Continuing along East Street, notice the rich variety of architectural styles which adorn the frontages, from the group of well proportioned three-storey Regency houses with their fine balcony fronts and railings to the pseudo Gothic of Number 70. Ireland House, number 53, is named after John Ireland, the son of an Ashburton butcher, who became the Dean of Westminster. He gave this building to Ashburton Grammar School, his old school, as a residence for the Headmaster together with a £1,000 endowment. The house was used as a boarding-house from 1845 to 1928.

Retrace your steps to Woodland Road past the fine portico and shopfront of W. G. Smith, Butcher, with its good clear lettering and delicacy of detail. Turn left along Woodland Road to Number 23 with its date and leaning wall.

Turn right past the Cattle Market where there is an annual sale of Dartmoor ponies held in October. The old Station, attributed to Brunel, is now a Garage and the old public house nearby used to be known as the Railway Inn and then, on closure of the line, The Silent Whistle, and latterly the Fleece and Firkin.

A right turn into St. Lawrence Lane leads to the Chapel of St. Lawrence (also the Old Grammar School) founded as a Chantry in 1314 by Bishop Stapledon. Here the annual Law Day of the Courts Leet and Baron is held. The Court Leet 67 originated in Saxon times and later became the Borough court. The town was governed by the Court Leet until 1894 when the Urban District Council was formed. The Court Baron is the Manor court to which the tenants could be elected. The courts meet together on the fourth Tuesday in November and elect such officers as Ale Tasters, Bread Weighers and Viewers of Water-courses. Some 1,160 Portreeves have now been in office.

Retrace your steps for fifty yards (46m) and turn right into narrow Blogishay Lane. The walls are rich in local limestone flora, notably spleenwort and rusty-back ferns. The river bed at the bridge is paved to prevent erosion. Follow the lane round to the Parish Church (well worth a visit) and out into West Street which has fine houses facing the Churchyard. A cockpit for cock-fighting existed behind Sparnham House. Walking down West Street you pass the Exeter Inn and Churchpath Arch, the Methodist Church and the Museum, once a brush factory.

Turn left into North Street. The ironmongers shop with granite archway was the Mermaid Inn where General Fairfax stayed on campaign in the Civil War. Further up is the 17th Century gaming house known as the Card House from the patterns on its slate hung facade. In the road about here was the Bull Ring.

On the left is the Kings Bridge and the Car Park.

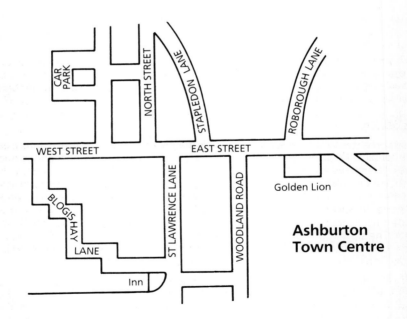

4½ miles (7.2 km), about 3 hours. Walk along the River Ashburn then climb to Whiddon for the views. Muddy near Whiddon in winter. Paths used: A2, A3, A19.

From the car park take Kingsbridge Lane over the bridge and at the Town Hall turn left along North Street. Approaching Great Bridge the road runs beside the River Ashburn. Look out for a flight of steps (R) starting from the road just before the bridge.

At the top of the steps a wide path, Terrace Walk, goes up the hill and our route, the footpath A2, branches immediately from this path and follows the contour near the bottom of the hill. The path passes above a bungalow (L) and then follows the Ashburn, where it is marked by stiles, to the metalled road near Cuddyford Bridge.

Cross the road to the kissing gate and take the left-hand path (A3) along the bottom of the field following the hedge (L).

Beyond the stile (and gate) the path continues along the bottom edge of Woodencliff Wood (R) by the fencing. The view across the meadows (L) is to Lurgecombe and the River Ashburn.

Lurgecombe has a long history as a mill. It was quite common for mills to fall out of use, become derelict, and then be rebuilt for a different purpose. In 1504 William Denbold paid 8d rent for a "smyth's mill in Loryggecombe" (probably a water powered tilt-hammer). In 1616 an 'ancient grist mill', one of four near the town, was recorded, and corn was also being ground there at the beginning of this century.

You soon enter Whiddon Scrubbs which is mainly an oak wood of standard trees and coppice. Until the beginning of this century it was the custom about once every twenty years to lease areas of the wood (and Boro Wood across the Ashburn) for coppicing. The poles were cut to the ground in the spring as the sap was rising and the oak bark was immediately ripped off and sold to the leather tanneries in Buckfastleigh. The brushwood was left lying until dry and was then made into faggots and sold as fuel to the townsfolk and used for thatching spars. The standard trees were left to mature until required for building timber. The wood is now owned by the National Park Authority which is re-establishing a traditional coppice with standards system of management.

Belford Mill can be seen across the Ashburn. It was the first mill served by the leat mentioned earlier. There has been a mill on this site from the 16th century at least. At an early date the building was converted from a corn mill into a fulling mill where the cloth straight from the looms was cleansed of grease (with Fuller's Earth) and then immersed in water and beaten to produce felting. The common local surname Tucker is said to originate with the workers at the 'Tucking Mills' as they were called.

A later reconstruction by Berry and Sons (woollen manufacturers and merchants) turned the building into a woollen mill; notice the weather boarding on the top storey where the fleeces would have been sorted before the combing began. By 1850 Berrys had moved to Buckfast to a bigger factory with more workers and Belford became a corn mill, its last operation.

Follow the Ashburn until you reach a lane where a ford and footbridge cross a tributary stream. Bear (R) up the lane A19 to Whiddon and Owlacombe Cross. At first the lane climbs quite steeply then follows the side of the hill to Whiddon. This last stretch can be muddy after rain. Behind you, as you climb, is Boro Wood (L) and the houses of Bowdley: the white house on the skyline is Welstor.

Upper and Lower Bowdley were tenements (freehold land as distinct from the common and leasehold lands of the Lord of the Manor) and part of the Borough of Ashburton. At Whiddon the lane runs between various farm buildings and dwellings, bearing to the R, and on the metalled road. Here turn right and then fork right on to the Ashburton road.

Passing Brownswell it will be noticed that Lower Brownswell, down the lane (L), is now ruined. From the next gate (L), beyond Brownswell, there is a clear view on to the limestone quarry. It has been an important source of lime for spreading on the acid soils of the moorland farms for several hundred years and supplies stone for building and road-making. Until about 10 years ago Ashburton Marble was also quarried from a particular bed of black limestone with pink streaks. Specimens are found in buidings all over the world and can be seen locally in the parish church and the kerb-stones in the town centre (a rosy variety). Cut and polished specimens are on show in Ashburton Museum.

Continue along the road. The footpath A2 starts at a kissing gate (R) half-way down Tower Hill. From the gate there is a skyline view (L to R) of Brent Hill (beyond Ashburton), Eastern Whittaborough with a large cairn on top, Pupers with 3 small tors, Snowdon with 3 cairns, Ryders Hill (at 1,691 feet (515 m) the highest point on southern Dartmoor), and Holne Ridge.

The footpath goes down the hill to the stile in the hedge just to the R of the gateway. From the stile cross the field to the kissing gate, right of the houses.

From here return as the outward route. (Alternatively, you could cross Cuddyford Bridge, fork left and left again at Rewe Cross for North Street.) From the stone stile follow the path by the Ashburn. When the third field is reached the path climbs away from the river passing just above the bungalow to the corner of the field. Take the flight of steps down into North Street (watch out for traffic), cross the road and turn left for the centre of Ashburton.

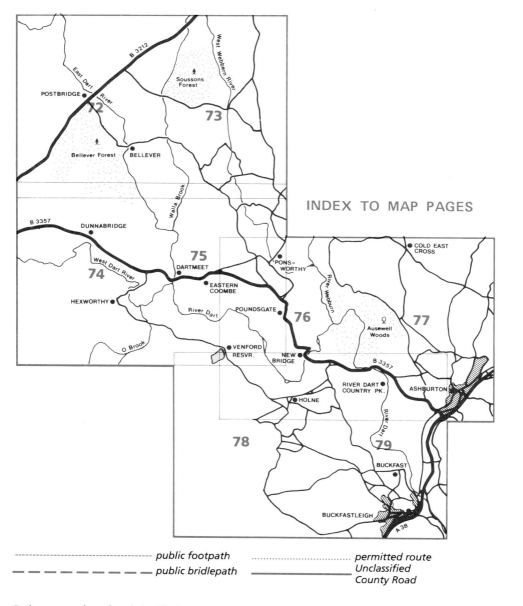

INDEX TO MAP PAGES

```
----------------------------- public footpath        ..................... permitted route
— — — — — — — — — — public bridlepath        ——————— Unclassified
                                                           County Road
```

Paths are numbered and classified according to what parish they are in.

These maps are to a scale of 2½″ to 1 mile, and are based on the Ordnance Survey Map with the permission of the Controller of H.M. Stationery Office.

Public rights of way shown on the maps are based on the County Definitive Map of Public Paths, and may be amended by later enactment or order.

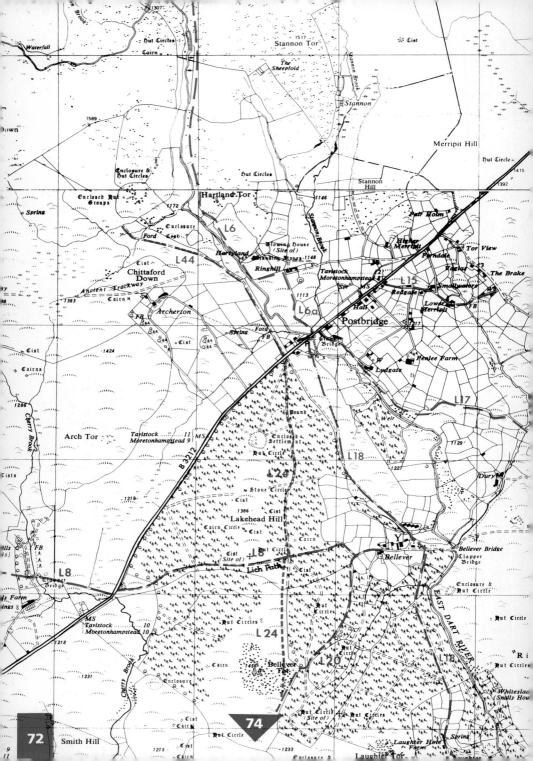

NOTES

[1] W. Crossing: "Amid Devonia's Alps", 1888. David and Charles, reprint 1974. Also entitled "Wanderings and Adventures on Dartmoor" – the most personal of Crossing's works.

[2] W. Crossing: "Dartmoor Worker", David and Charles, 1966. A reprint of articles appearing in the Western Morning News from 1903.

[3] W. Crossing: "Guide to Dartmoor". First appeared in 1909 and is still the best guide to the moor. David and Charles, reprint 1965, also contains an account of William Crossing's life.

[4] Crispin Gill (ed.): "Dartmoor: A New Study", David and Charles, 1970. A survey of the historical development and present-day status of Dartmoor. The development of farming is given by a detailed study of Babeny Farm, one of the oldest of the ancient tenements.

[5] R. Hansford Worth: "Dartmoor". David and Charles, 1967.

[6] W. Crossing: "Gems in a Granite Setting", 1905.

[7] W. Crossing: "Hundred Years on Dartmoor", 1901. David and Charles, reprint 1967. An account of life on Dartmoor in the 19th century.

[8] W. Crossing: "The Ancient Stone Crosses of Dartmoor and its Borderland", 1902.

[9] A. Fleming: "The Dartmoor Reaves", Current Archaeology No. 55, 1977.

[10] A. Fleming: "Dartmoor Reaves: a 19th century fiasco", Antiquity 52, 1978. A history of the archaeological ideas concerning reaves.

[11] A. Fleming and J. Collis: "A late prehistoric reave system near Cholwich Town, Dartmoor". Proceedings of the Devon Archaeological Society, 31, 1973.

E. Gawne and J. Somers Cocks: "Parallel reaves on Dartmoor", Trans Devonshire Assoc. 100, 1965. These two articles led to the founding of the Dartmoor Reave Project.

[12] A. Fleming: "The prehistoric landscape of Dartmoor. Part 1: South Dartmoor". Proceedings of the Prehistoric Society 44, 1978.

[13] To commemorate the Silver Jubilee of Queen Elizabeth II, the reminiscences of some of the local people have been recorded in a booklet called "A History of Holne".

[14] The history of the Abbey and surrounding lands are described in the book "A History of Buckfast Abbey from 1018 to 1968", by Dom John Stephan, Burleigh Press, Bristol, 1970.

[15] This walk is taken, with only minor changes, from "Devon Town Trails" published by Devon County Council in 1975. The Ashburton Amenity Society compiled the trail for that town.

[16] The Pengelly Trust Caves are only open to the public by special appointment.

[17] Peter Teal: "Hand Woolcombing and Spinning. A Guide to Worsteds from the Spinning Wheel", Blandford Press, Dorset, 1976. A comprehensive book based on the author's own practical knowledge, and studies of early manuscripts and industrial techniques.

[18] Dr. Francis Pilkington: "Ashburton. The Dartmoor Town". 1978.

[19] W. R. Hatch: "Ashburton Museum: Twenty years of Local effort". The Devon Historian, Vol. 13, 1976. This article by the Honorary Curator can be bought from the Museum as a leaflet, price 5p.

[13] Tom Greaves: "Tin Mines and Miners of Dartmoor". Devon Books, 1986.